Turning t

Cycling from Land's End to

ROSS P LORAM

Published by Angrygerbil Publishing

ISBN: 099309211X
ISBN-13: 978-0993092114

DEDICATION

To Poodle.

CONTENTS

1 THE TERRIBLE FIRST ATTEMPT

"Bloody hell mate! You alright?!?" cries the shocked Scottish guy, winding down his van window as he screeches to a halt beside me.

"Yea sure, no problem" I wince, as I try to understand what just happened.

"Glad to hear it, that was some hit!" he says with an impressed air before driving on.

"Yea, sure was" I manage as he drives off. With the van out of sight, I began to ask myself if I really was okay. I don't know why, but my brain automatically jumps to a default reaction of thinking everything is okay after an accident. It might be the same for everyone, or I might be a bit strange. Well, there's no doubting I'm a bit strange, but I digress. It's like when you fall over in front of a group of people, you automatically bounce back up and make it around the corner before collapsing into a heap, or realising you're bleeding profusely. Well that's just how I react to everything. So, with the van out of sight I looked around me. I was in the middle of the road and underneath my pushbike somehow. I seemed to have a few small cuts to my legs and arms, and a severely dodgy feeling elbow. I remembered landing on that. Hmm, probably best to get out of the road.

Crawling out from underneath the bike wasn't terribly easy, as it was loaded up with heavy panniers, and still had a trailer attached to the back of it. Standing up in the deserted road, I looked down at my damaged arm and my damaged bike, then I realised that my Guardians of the Galaxy soundtrack was still blaring out of the speaker attached to my handlebars. I laughed. Ow! That hurt, don't laugh. Okay, what next? Probably get the bike out of the road. I couldn't seem to get the bike upright due to its weight and loading, but did manage to sort of drag it into the long grass verge to the side of the road, once there I leaned in to take a closer look. Most of the bike seemed to be okay, all the panniers protecting it from the crash quite nicely. The front seemed to be the only problem area, with the handlebars at a 45 degree angle to the front wheels, well they should straighten out, and one end of the handlebars including the brake and gear levers bent around on itself. Putting one hand on the straight part of the bars and one on the bent piece, I attempted to pull them back to at least somewhere near straight. Nothing happened. Hmm, seemed like I should be able to bend that. Turning my attention away from the bike, I began looking at what I'd done to myself. I remembered struggling with the crosswinds before the crash. The single wheel trailer I'd brought with me for the tour had been a bad idea, strapping a flat sided pop up tent to the side of it had been an even worse idea, as in it's packed form it was incredibly good at catching the winds. I'd only been gone a little while, but I'd nearly turned back more than once to ditch the trailer. Why hadn't I turned back? Stubborn man. I shook my head and looked down the perfectly straight road I'd just been cycling along. Completely open for miles to either side, this far north in Scotland was known for its strong winds and they'd just bitten me. I'd only been doing about 15mph, but a big gust had started to get me into a bit of a wobble, and then slightly more of a wobble, until eventually I think the trailer had been blown over as much as the pivot to the bike would allow, so that when it kept trying to be blown over even more, it took the bike with it. It had all happened very quickly, but I definitely remember the bars snapping left as the bike blew over, and thus effectively stopping. I'd ditched my normal pedals for the tour, the ones that keep you attached to the bike, the reason you see cyclists trying desperately not to stop at red lights, to save unclicking and then re-clicking back to their pedals. Instead my bike was fitted with traditional pedals. As a result, when the bike abruptly slowed, I didn't, instead carrying right on going over the handlebars, and landing with all my weight on that left elbow that didn't seem to be playing ball any more. The bike then used what little momentum it had left, to continue on a few feet before landing on me. Helpful. I tried to straighten my left arm and found it wouldn't. It also wasn't too keen on bending much either, plus there was now a massive lump that looked like the heel of your foot, sticking out behind my elbow. That didn't look good, and I was sure it hadn't been that bad a couple minutes ago. S**t. I couldn't be injured, I had to be okay, had to carry on.

The rest of me did still seem to be okay, much to my delight. A little bleeding from my knees and hands but not too much, which was a good thing as I'm truly terrible around blood, or even the talk of it. I am one of the most squeamish people you'll ever meet, genuinely not even making it through a Biology lesson at school, without turning white as a ghost and having to leave the classroom before fainting. Fun times. So yes, not too much blood, that was good. Although I do seem to be able to keep my head together better in an emergency, but otherwise, no, don't come to me with stories of cuts, blood loss or medical procedures. No no no.

Sitting down in the grass verge, I pulled my phone out of its holder on the handlebars, thinking it was a minor miracle that it hadn't been smashed to pieces. I stared at it not being sure what to do first. Apparently I rang Dad. I have no memory of the phone call, but he did turn up a little later so it's hard to argue that I didn't. He, and Mum, were only 8 miles away, having just dropped me to John O'Groats to start my long tour south, all the way to Land's End. They had planned to spend a couple weeks touring around Scotland in the campervan, while I continued south, aiming to cross something off my bucket list that had been there for far too long. The legendary John O'Groats to Land's End cycle. This trip had been months in the planning. I'd been out training every weekend, not huge amounts but a solid sixty to eighty miles each Sunday morning for the previous few months. I'd tested my equipment, trained carrying it for the final few ride outs even. Routes had been thoroughly researched, before finally settling on a great 'traffic free' one that another cyclist had devised a few years earlier, after he got frustrated at seeing cyclists using so many dangerous roads to complete the trip. I'm in full agreement of this, and try to avoid busy roads as much as possible, so his route seemed right up my street. At 1200 miles it was much longer than most of the alternative routes, but if it kept me safe it was worth it. Plus I'd saved up my holidays and had the full month of July to complete the journey. Plenty of time to really enjoy it, not rush, but be able to stop when somewhere took my fancy, take photos, videos, treat it as a break rather than just an endurance challenge. I was raising money for the Teenage Cancer Trust, who I would also be competing for at Ride London, on my return right at the end of July. I'd announced my plans loudly and widely to everyone I knew months in advance, setting off from John O'Groats with everyone knowing I was on my way, thanks to my big mouth and Facebook post to tell them. And now here I was, 8 miles into a month long, 1200 mile trip, sat on the grass verge, with a broken bike, an elbow that wouldn't move, and a phone getting progressively more covered in blood as I handled it. I wiped it clean and stared at it, before opening my camera and pressing record. Of course I did. Idiot. What I did film has been seen by two people, and that is all who will ever see it. Several minutes of me, clearly in shock and not making any sense, mumbling away that everything just had to be okay, it couldn't not be, whilst simply stating, "I don't know what I've done…" at least 10 times. It's as hilarious as it is tragic and cringe worthy. But there was some truth, I genuinely didn't know what I'd done!

A few minutes later, and I was feeling much more myself again when my phone rang. It was Mum, checking to see where I was, and knowing her, making sure that I was still conscious. Apparently I hadn't been very descriptive when I'd spoken to Dad, just saying I'd crashed and the bike was stuffed, over and over. I still don't remember that call. I described my elbow to Mum, who has worked in care her whole life and has seen most injuries. Broken she said, definitely broken, without taking so much as a look at it. Nope, I replied, unacceptable, it just couldn't be, I still had 1192 miles to go. I don't like being beaten.

Fast forward a few minutes and the parents arrived in our familiar campervan, a welcome sight. I began pointing out to Dad what had happened to the bike, while Mum fussed around me and looked horrified at the state of my elbow, which admittedly by this point was pretty dodgy looking. Me and the bike were bundled into the camper and the sat nav was programmed for the nearest hospital, Thurso. Only around 10 miles away, but it felt like longer. On arrival it didn't look so much a hospital as a school or village hall, but once inside two of the nicest, most confidence inspiring, and straight talking nurses set to work. They cleaned up my various cuts and grazes, picking several bits of gravel and debris out that I'd missed, before covering them over. Turning attention to my elbow next and this was up for debate. Without an X-Ray machine available, it was left to experience and instinct to determine how badly damaged it was. I was asked to straighten my arm, bend it, hold it over my head, do all sorts of things really. I managed most of them, although did admit to it not being comfortable. The nurse, with years of experience behind her, watched all these movements with eagle eyes, as well as feeling the elbow and staring at it very closely. She thought that I may just have very bad swelling. If it was no better in the morning then I had to go to the hospital in Wick to get it X-rayed, otherwise it would be a case of time. Yes! I thought, this is fantastic! I've got a month off work, I can send the parents off on their trip, while I hide out at John O'Groats for a few days while this calms down. Why I could even spend a week up here and still have three weeks for the trip, that's manageable, this is totally fine……. yes it'll be okay …….. what's going to be okay? …….. where am I again? …….

……"Ross? Ross can you hear me now? Yes he's coming round now. You just passed out there for a minute"

I opened my eyes with a start, my whole body jolted and I found Mum's face staring into mine, with the nurse stood behind her. I'd been having this nightmare that I'd messed up my trip on day one…..bugger. The nurse continued speaking, "Don't worry dear, happens all the time, I hear you're a bit squeamish and there was a lot of that talk going on, but don't you worry, we'll get some sweet tea and some biscuits down you and you'll be fine." I was relieved my squeamishness was getting the blame, not that I'd just been trying to do exercises that weren't terribly comfortable to me. Soon enough the second nurse appeared with tea and shortbread, a combination to make your teeth curl, but it did the trick and I was free to go ten minutes later. Not feeling terribly macho you understand but free to go!

As it was now early evening, we retreated to the campsite at John O'Groats for an early night. After taking a couple Ibuprofen to help with the swelling, it was time to settle down to a disturbed nights sleep, where I'd wake myself up constantly as I tried to roll onto the bad arm. Come morning I'd had very little sleep, and my arm was feeling much much worse. And completely immovable without screaming. Well this wasn't the plan at all! So, for the second day in succession we set off for a hospital, Wick being the destination this time.

With Wick being a bigger town, the hospital looked far more like something you're used to seeing, with the amount of people you're used to seeing too! With that in mind it was a 3 hour wait until they had chance to give me an X-ray. Massively amusingly everything then happened very quickly, as they took one look at the X-rays and pushed me to the front of all the queues. A doctor appeared to tell me that I would in no way be going near a pushbike for some time, as my elbow was quite badly broken, an Olecranon fracture being the technical term. I was told I'd need surgery to fix this (basically a large plate securing the parts together) and that it would be unwise to travel all the way home to Devon for it. Instead I was to be put in a temporary cast to keep anything else from moving (lets ignore the gymnastics I was performing the previous day, trying to convince the nurse I was fine!) while I travelled to Raigmore Hospital in Inverness for the operation. Couldn't the operation be done here? Oh no, we don't do operations that large here. The doctor hurried off to prepare some paperwork while my arm was wrapped for the trip. I was gutted. All that planning, preparation, fanfare, and it was over before it had begun, I felt like such an idiot. Because everyone knew when I started they were all expecting updates, so I had to own up to the crash, and now that I wouldn't be continuing any time soon either. I had a major funk on.

Arm now wrapped and held steady, and with paperwork in hand, we headed off to Inverness, another 100 miles or so. Honestly, if you live in a reasonably connected area as most of us do, then don't take your local hospital for granted, hurting yourself somewhere more remote really brings home how lucky we are most of the time!

Tuesday night and we arrived at Raigmore Hospital, this trip was rapidly turning into a tour of Scotland's Hospitals! After going through all the paperwork (getting quite used to the process by this point) and speaking with several doctors on the Wednesday morning, I was all ready for the operation in the afternoon. I'd never had a general anaesthetic before, much less an actual operation, but as far as I was concerned I'd go to sleep broken and wake up fixed, simple! It was an odd feeling as the mask was placed on my face, and I was asked to count backwards from ten. I giggled to myself that it's the sort of thing you see on TV and in films all the time, but now it was for real. I was only trying to cycle from one end to the other, how had it gone so wrong, I wonder how far……

"……that's it. Everything's okay, you're just waking up a bit groggy is all. It happens sometimes, the anaesthetic just doesn't agree with some people." I opened my eyes to see another unfamiliar room, lots of empty beds opposite me, and a nurse beside me who gave me the impression I'd half come round, before drifting off again several times. Opening my mouth I found I couldn't come up with a question, this was very confusing. "Right, we're going to wheel you back up to the ward now." With that two more people came across, whisking me and the bed away. I felt so hot, hotter than I'd ever felt before. And sick, I was definitely going to be sick. Make this bed stop moving. Please. My ability to speak seemed to have vanished. We entered a lift, a lift that left my stomach several floors below, before we were back onto the floor and ward I'd been in earlier, my bed and me wheeled into place as the nurses on the ward took slightly startled glances at me. I did look awful. Felt worse. The parents were there of course, looking worried as the operation had taken over twice as long as expected, due in part to the arm, and partly me being rubbish at waking up from anaesthetic. "Take my socks off" were the first words I managed to mumble since waking up, "too hot" as I struggled to throw the blankets off, surprised that my arm was massive, wrapped up and largely useless. Of course, that's why I was here. The nurses were adamant I was cold, and I was adamant I was about to catch fire and feeling pretty irritated at the whole situation. In the end we settled on blankets on, but a small fan blowing some air over my face. That felt better. I dozed off and on for a while apparently, occasionally asking a stupid question, while Dad took a photo of me looking ridiculous and drugged out of my head. Thanks Dad.

Feeling slightly more normal a couple hours later, I decided I was hungry. It was dinnertime after all and I hadn't eaten all day. One look at the dinner and I was sick, which in turn set the guy off in the bed opposite who was also sick. Great mealtime for everyone else, sorry chaps! Everything (arm excluded) felt normal apart from the sickness, but looking back at a couple messages I sent that evening, it's clear I still wasn't quite right! By midnight I'd managed some dry toast and I woke the next day feeling, and acting, like me again, what a relief!

It took some time during the morning to get checked over and get the medications ready etc, so it was mid-afternoon before they finally set me free. But what a relief to be out! The only slight annoyance was still being over 600 miles from home, not a particularly pleasing thought when you've just had a lump of metal screwed into your arm! We made it down to Ben Nevis by the evening, only 70 miles but 70 miles of the slowest little winding roads imaginable. As I've said I'm a squeamish person, so I was getting worried by this point by the amount of swelling in my upper arm and hand. Basically above and below my bandaging. It just felt much too tight. Trying to put it out of my mind as much as possible, I had some of my medication and settled in for another rubbish nights sleep.

The following day was spent travelling all the way home to Devon, whilst worrying about the swelling and purple appearance of my skin. We did consider stopping at a hospital on the way, very nearly did in fact, but decided to continue on and get it checked out at home. With it being Friday night when we did arrive home, that plan hastily got changed to a Saturday morning hospital visit. Friday night at Torbay A&E? No thanks!

So, cue another uncomfortable nights sleep followed by another hospital visit, although at least this time I knew the hospital. After getting the arm re-bandaged a little looser I was sent home. Although the swelling and dodgy colour did worry me and anyone who saw it, I at least knew that the professionals had seen it and deemed it okay, I just tried not to look at it too much. So, one week after leaving home, full of hope and ambition, I was back. Dad helped me in with the bike and all my unused supplies before heading home. I sat down on the sofa, let out a sigh and checked my calendar for my next holiday leave....I couldn't be beaten that easily.

2 A STUPID PLAN FAILS

The time after the crash was very, very frustrating. I'm not normally ill and I've never been injured in any way for a length of time. And now I was. I was not liking it. I'm a strange mix of a very lazy and a very active person. If something needs doing I like to crack on and get it done. I don't like asking for help. But similarly I can just lose a day if I have nothing to do, flicking between Movies, TV shows, Youtube, Facebook, WhatsApp or a book. But that's the odd day, not weeks of it. I was now going to be off work for at least a month. This was a long time! Especially as I'm a Postie so I'm used to getting exercise, like it or not!

I'd been told that the arm had to be 'non weight bearing' for 10 to 12 weeks, which felt like a massive amount of time. Frustratingly, I'd just moved into a new house a few months before the trip, and although I'd pretty much finished renovating it there were still jobs to be done, but they couldn't be done one handed. As it was I knew I was probably doing a little too much with the arm, although I did try not to massively overdo it, just to keep it moving as much as possible, to try and get back as much movement as possible.

Over time the arm was improving, and I began to plot when I could get back on my bike. An appointment at Torbay Hospital was arranged on July 10th, so just under 2 weeks after the crash, to check on my progress. Happily everything looked good (except for my purple druggie looking appearance) and my bandages were removed, showering would be so much easier! Another plus point had been Dad lending me his Jag. Now, I really don't like his old Jag, but it is an automatic which meant I could drive again! Yay! Improvements everywhere, even if everyone laughed at my 'old man's car'. Thanks Dad. Back at home I rigged the bike up on my turbo trainer (basically a device that lets you cycle your bike indoors like an exercise bike) and that evening, July 10th, turned the pedals for the first time since the crash. It felt strange, knowing I should still have been heading towards Land's End at this point, but I was plotting a comeback. A stupid comeback. Just my style!

You know when you have an idea, and it's a stupid idea, and even though you know it's stupid you want to do it anyway? Yes? What do you mean no? Well, I had a stupid idea and it was already on my calendar. Ride London. I'd been looking forward to it for months. My friend Rob had already completed Ride

London a few times, and I'd been massively jealous of him. If you've never heard of it, it's a completely closed road 100 mile sportive around the streets of London. It's televised, the pros have their own races, and the main sportive that I'd entered has over 20,000 riders. I had my place, my rider number and didn't want to give them up. I managed maybe 20 minutes on the turbo trainer that first time since the crash, but I wasn't being silly just yet, sitting upright, not putting any weight down through my arm.

For a few days I kept this up, doing a little more each time and really noticing that I'd done little exercise for a few weeks. I'd adjusted my position on the bike as much as possible, to enable me to hold the handlebars without leaning forwards as much as normal, hence putting as little weight through my arm as possible. I kept this up for a couple more days, effectively carrying my weight through my good right arm, my left arm really just resting on the bars. I began, in my deluded brain that really can't accept being beaten, to think that this was achievable. My only worry was another crash. I'd been told that after a month the bone healing would be rather like jelly, and if knocked heavily it would be very difficult to put right. I told myself some rubbish that I'd bandage up, wear an elbow pad and just not crash. I could see this was stupid but I couldn't stop myself. Mum and Dad were livid. My best friend told me I was an idiot. Couldn't really argue with any of them, they were right of course, but I just couldn't fail at something else! In the end I did see sense and threw the towel in, withdrawing from the event. Very depressing. The bike and the turbo trainer were pushed back into the corner, with neither being used for several months. I spent the day of Ride London ignoring the TV coverage and bikes in general, instead spending the day with my friend who had helped me make the right decision, thanks muchly.

3 THE SECOND ATTEMPT

I don't remember when I decided on the second attempt, but it wasn't long before I left. I returned to work in early August, not my usual outdoor Postie job but instead working indoors in our delivery office, answering phones, doing paperwork, dealing with customers etc. Hated it. Hated every damn minute of it. My previous job had been office based and this was bringing back how much I disliked it. Within a few weeks I'd managed to largely bin the office off and get back to my usual job, albeit rather carefully. My arm was still a bit of an issue, it always will be to some extent, but it was becoming more useable, and as we entered into September I realised I had two weeks annual leave booked for the first two weeks of October. Hmm, 14 free days. No, 15 free days as I'd have the Sunday October 1st off before my leave started. Scratch that, 16 free days, as my rotation happened to have me off on Saturday 30th September too. I'd crashed at the very end of June and been told to stay off my bike for 3 months. This was 3 months to the day. I don't think the doctors meant, stay off your bike for 3 months but then you're free to cycle 1200 miles in a fortnight, but they hadn't said that, so I reasoned I wasn't breaking their rules! I could do this I thought. I could right a wrong and get it right this time!

By mid-September I'd all but sold this latest stupid idea to myself, to the point where I'd booked a train from home to Penzance for Friday night after work, and then a train at the other end to get me from Wick (near John O'Groats) to Inverness, and a hire car so I could drive from Inverness to home. The reasoning behind starting from Land's End, was firstly that the prevailing wind direction is northerly, so it just makes sense, plus if I realised I wasn't fit enough then I'd be cycling past my front door a couple days into the trip. Perfect sense. I ordered some front panniers for the bike (no the trailer would not be coming with me again) and stole some of my Uncles rather good camping gear, to mix with my own. A lot of the 'luxury items' that I had planned to take with me the first time got binned off, which just about allowed me to fit everything into my four panniers. Excellent. If you're planning a trip, here's the full list of items I took, including everything I was wearing when I left –

The bike itself –

B'twin Triban 3 Road Bike, modified with Shimano Rs11 Wheelset, Continental GP4000 Tyres and Inner Tubes, Brooks Touring Saddle, Kool Stop Brake

Blocks, lightweight front and rear racks, panniers and top tube bag.

The equipment –

2 lightweight sleeping bags, packed inside a compression sack, inside a lightweight dry bag. (Bear in mind I was doing this in October, you could manage with one in the summer) Quechua Pop Up Tent. (The finest easiest tent ever made, buy one) Sleeping mat.

2 sets of Lycra. 1 Pair of Jogging Bottoms. 2 T-shirts. 2 Jumpers. 1 Pair of waterproof trousers. 1 waterproof cycling jacket. 3 Pairs of ankle socks. One Pair of hiking shoes. (Again, you could manage with less in the summer)

1 Microfibre Towel. Toothpaste and Toothbrush. Tub of Assos Chamois Crème. Assos Skin Repair Gel. Plasters. Wet wipes. Suncream. Toilet Roll.

3 Inner Tubes. 1 tyre. Tyre levers. Puncture Repair Kit. Multi-tool. Spare Q/R Skewer. Chain. Chain Tool. Cable Ties. Tank tape. (Failing all else you can fix anything with cable ties and tank tape!)

Lightweight camping stove and pan set. Camping gas. Many dried pasta and rice meals. (The 'add water' types) Teabags. Sugar. Spork. 2 800ml Cycling Drinks Bottles. 2 500ml Drinks bottles.

Phone (Used for phone calls, messaging, navigation,

Googling campsites, B&B's etc) Two High Capacity Battery Packs (To recharge phone) Small Go-Pro style camera.

Debit Card. Small amount of cash.

Lucky Mascot!

So, with a rough plan in place for getting myself to and from the start and finish points, as well as having gathered together everything I hoped I'd need for the trip, things were looking good. It was by now mid-September and learning from my previous mistake, and wishing to do things a little bit more 'low key' this time, there would be no large Facebook announcements about my plans, nor would they be shouted from the rooftops. One week before my planned departure and I took the bike out onto the roads for the first time since the crash nearly 3 months earlier. It had also been 2 months since I'd even ridden the thing on the turbo trainer, this really was such a terrible idea! Leaving my house early on a Sunday morning, I cycled up the Teign Valley to our garage just outside Ide, had a quick cuppa with my friend Paul, then cycled back again. It's about a 30 mile round trip, and save for one big hill near the garage it's reasonably flat. Feeling okay at the end of it, I reasoned I was absolutely fine to now attempt 1200 miles in a fortnight! They say the best memories come from bad ideas after all.

A few of the guys from work knew about my trip, but apart from them, my best friend, my parents and one of two other family members, nobody else knew. My boss is a keen cyclist and knew about my plans, he deemed me an absolute lunatic to be attempting it on no training and demanded I write the book of such a mad idea… well here you go Richie!

The week leading up to the second attempt was very busy, with an immense amount of rushing to get everything ready before leaving. I also nearly drowned the weekend before, and not in a dramatic 'I swallowed a bit of water' nearly drowned, I mean properly thought my number was up, had to be dragged back to the surface by a friend nearly drowned. Safe to say nerves were slightly on edge already then!

As the week wore on, so did my endless list of jobs. The parents had been away for the previous few weeks, but handily they were back the day before I was due to leave, as such they'd been given my cat Luna to look after until my return. With her gone on Thursday night, I finished up the last of my packing and grabbed a few hours sleep before getting up for work the next morning, excited and daunted by the challenge that lay ahead. Not a lot of thought went into the job that day and I was glad to finish, get home, and get myself sorted out ready to cycle the few miles from my house to Newton Abbot Train station. I reasoned on the way to the station that this particular road at rush hour, was likely to be the dodgiest I'd have to contend with for some time!

Thankfully after making it to the station without

any dramas (how embarrassing would that have been!) I found my way to the right platform. In truth Newton Abbot station is not big, but I don't get trains often and never with a bike before, so the whole process was a bit alien to me. I was slightly disturbed to find that I'd have to load the bike up myself, having naively thought that would get taken care of for me, but apparently not. Still, I was here, a little early but better than being late, and ready for an adventure. Well no, I wasn't really ready, but I'd been ready last time and look how badly that had gone. This was much more of a 'wing and a prayer' type of adventure, improvise and make do, it wouldn't be comfortable but it had to be worth a go. I sent a few messages and waited for the train. Finally an announcement came that it was due in a few minutes, and that the cycle carriage was at the front of the train. Perfect. Except I didn't know which direction it was coming from. Hedging my bets, I waited in the middle of the impossibly long platform. When the train came into view, I began zig zagging my way through the sea of people that suddenly seemed to have materialised out of thin air, towards the front carriage. The train had already been stopped a few seconds by the time I made it, and heaved the heavy bike up the step onto the carriage. A couple bikes already stood in racks to the sides, so I wedged my bike, named 'Bants', in the middle, and hurried to secure the front wheel with one of the velcro straps hanging down. I was flustered, in a rush, and the strap was next to useless. I was also out of time. Crossing my fingers that the bike would stay put, I jumped out of the carriage. (No access to passenger carriages from the bike carriage) Back on the platform I realised everyone else was already on board, and all the doors looked to be shut. A horrifying image flashed before me, of standing there and watching my bike disappear off into Cornwall without me, never to be seen again. I literally ran towards the first door I saw and was incredibly relieved to be able to yank it open and step aboard. I had a reserved seat but the train was absolutely packed, and I had no idea where it was. In the end I settled for any empty seat, so long as I was on the train with my bike and heading in the right direction, that was fine by me!

With my heart racing, I settled back into my seat, a rather plusher comfier seat than imagined, as the train set off. Looking around me revealed an odd mix of young, old, retired, posh, common, just about any class or age of person you could think of. It seems trains are for all. Seated a couple rows in front of me on the opposite side of the carriage, was the most stereotypical businessman you ever saw. If you searched Google for a stock image of a 'businessman' then this guy is who would appear. Sprawled out on the table in front of him were his laptop, tablet, mobile, as well as several folders and various paperwork. I'm all for getting a bit of work done, or doing something to pass the journey, but this guy was taking it to ridiculous levels. Through it all, he also managed to somehow maintain an air of utter defiance and contempt that the rest of us seemed to be in his 'office'. I was almost sad when he got off in Plymouth, he'd been a good source of amusement.

As we headed further south the train became very quiet, just a few of us to a carriage. After sending a few excited texts to the few people who knew what I was up to, I decided to pop my headphones in, close my eyes, and listen to one of the audiobooks I'd downloaded to my phone in preparation for any dull parts of my trip. As the train glided further into Cornwall, I lost myself in the wonderfully geeky world depicted by Ernest Cline in 'Ready Player One', as read by Will Wheaton apparently, which was a little odd but it beat staring at the back of the seat in front.

I think I had a little doze. It'd been a busy week without much sleep, and we suddenly seemed nearer to Penzance than I imagined we would be. It turns out I'd also misread the train times in my mad rush to prepare everything, so we arrived in Penzance, the 'end of the line', at 8:40pm. Great news, I thought we were getting here at 10pm! Jumping off the train I hurried towards the cycle area at the front, pulling open the door and letting out a massive sigh as 'Bants' the bike was still there in all his glory, awaiting the adventure ahead of him. I eagerly bumped him down onto the platform, wheeled him out of the station into the cold dark night, before flicking the lights on, pulling my helmet on, and stepping over the crossbar ready to leave. Hmm, where was I going again? I've never done a cycle tour before, never not known where I was going. Sure I've done Sportives and events in areas unfamiliar to me, but in those cases you're part of a large group, and the route is all signed anyway. I didn't expect to find too many signs labelled 'This way Ross' during the next 1200 miles. Taking my phone out, I fixed it onto its holder on my handlebars (the same one that had done such a good job of securing it during my crash last time) and entered the postcode for my pre-booked campsite. The Google Maps app confirmed that the distance was around 8 miles as expected, the route flashed up on screen and I selected 'cycle'. I was ready to go. I pushed off and followed the little arrow on my screen, which quickly took me straight along Penzance seafront. This was amazing I thought to myself as I cycled along. The cool crisp sea air, being somewhere new, doing something different and alone. A proper against the odds real adventure….

I'm going to veer off and tell you a little about myself now. To maybe try and explain why I decided to go and cycle from Land's End to John O'Groats in the first place, seeing as that's a question I've been asked countless times. So here goes……I'm a strange man. I won't deny that. As I passed that milestone of a birthday a couple years back, the big 30, I realised I was unhappy. Single, living with my parents, in the same job for some time, skint, and as much as I loved my major hobby and pastime, motor racing, it was severely pissing me off and was also the number one reason why I was skint, and thus living with my parents. Not that I don't get on with my parents, we have a very good relationship, but still, a guy into your 30's and living at home, not a good thing really. I realised things had to change. But I'm a shy coward, so they didn't. A year later and approaching my 31st birthday I gave myself the same talk. What had changed? Nothing much, that's what. I'd published my first book, a little take on my love of motorsport in December 2014, but that had been the only thing I'd crossed off my bucket list since turning 30. I needed more. I needed changes. First thing to go was the motor racing. That devastated and freed me in equal parts. I'd grown up with racing, Dad had raced since I was a child, and at the age of 23 (no I don't know why I left it so late) I jumped in his car, won at my first meeting and never looked back. After winning a couple local oval track championships in my first 2 seasons, we then headed out onto the big circuits, Brands Hatch, Silverstone etc. It was a huge adventure, we had nowhere near enough money to do it, but me and Dad put all we had into it, both in time and money terms, built and rebuilt the cars (mostly Dad there on the fabrication front) and kept relentlessly trying and trying again, until we became pretty competitive. 2014 had been my best year in motorsport I felt. We'd raced all over the country in a very competitive championship, in our home built car, always being somewhere near the front, finishing top 5 in the championship. I'd been driving the wheels off that car all year. But that's the thing that pissed me off about motorsport. I knew how much we were spending, and although it was everything we had, it was nothing compared to the other guys budgets. We'd beaten most of them, but not all of them, and call me cocky but I just know in equal cars I wouldn't have feared any of them. Anyway, introduce me to a racing driver who isn't a bit cocky and I'll introduce you to a loser. At the end of the season everyone went away and stretched their budgets, one blew a few million on a move to the British Touring Car

Championship, another told me he tried 17 engines during the previous season. Everyone else spent more and more developing their cars, and amid a start of the next season plagued with technical difficulties I felt like it was becoming more and more of a struggle not to slide back down the grid. This would be one thing, but spending every single penny and moment of time on this was stopping me doing anything else. Something had to give and it happened at the Lydden Hill circuit just before my 31st birthday. After a poor first race, where I just couldn't get the car to do what I'd like it to, and a technical problem in the second, I called enough. I'd made my decision before I'd driven back to the pits. I'd been close to it for some time and now I knew for certain. That was it. Everyone was very shocked but I just knew. It was a shame to lose something that me and Dad had done together for so long but I think he got it, and he did start racing again himself a while after.

With the racing over, my attention turned to what else I wanted to do. I wanted a house. Right then. I did own a flat in Dawlish so that was sold, I worked all the hours under the sun, pulled all my money together and began looking for a house just after my 32nd birthday. After several viewings and close calls, I found one I liked a few months later. Perhaps not the finest of areas as I'd have liked, but it was detached which appealed to me and I certainly didn't want to buy a flat. With the contracts complete, I got the keys and spent several months absolutely gutting the place and starting again, getting it to my liking. It was furnished and I moved in several months before my first unsuccessful Land's End to John O'Groats attempt, and my 33rd birthday. I'm pleased to say I've been happy living in my new house and I'm continuing to change my life. It's not where I want it to be yet, some things have depressed me more than I thought possible, and I'm not where I'd like to be as a person yet, but I'm getting better. I'm more sociable, I've learnt a lot of new skills, hell I can even cook a half decent meal these days! It's in the spirit of having these new experiences, and crossing things off my bucket list that have been gathering dust for too long, that I decided to do this trip. I'm a bit slow in realising life is short, just get out there and do whatever the hell you want. And that's why I found myself cycling along Penzance seafront, in the dark at 9pm on Friday 29th September 2017, with a metal plate in my arm, a smile on my face and only a vague idea of the challenges that lay ahead. Perfect.

After stopping for a quick photo on the seafront I pedalled on, hoping to get a reasonably early night. My directions took me along the length of the seafront, through a small section of town, and then down a very dark lane which seemed to connect with a cycle path that would allow me to carry on along the seafront. Struggling to see in the dark and rather cursing that I didn't buy some better lights for the trip, I could just make out a gate in front of me. Closer inspection revealed that it had been padlocked shut. Excellent. A small notice had also been stuck to the gate.

'BEACH CLOSED DUE TO PORTUGESE

MEN O'WAR BEING WASHED UP ON THE BEACH. STAY CLEAR. DANGER'

What? I thought to myself. Followed shortly after by, what? Portugese men of war? What war? What were the Cornish on about? I shook my head for the first of many times during my trip, selected a different 'by road' route on my phone, turned around and set off again. It was only the next day that a quick Google search revealed to me that 'Portugese Men O'war' are a deadly Jellyfish like creature, (or hydrozoan if you'd like to get technical) which had been washed up on the beach in unprecedented numbers during the previous few days. Literally hundreds per day. So if you take nothing else from this book, take away that little bit of marine knowledge.

Back to my Friday night detour and after climbing up honestly the steepest little winding road I've ever seen, I left the houses and streetlights of Penzance behind me, and headed off into the empty countryside towards my campsite. Oh dear, I really should have bought some better lights….this was horrendous. The lack of streetlights was bad, the thick cloud blocking out any moonlight was worse. I crawled along, worried I was going to smash into a hole hidden in the darkness, or just plain miss a turn in the road, it was absolutely hopeless. At least I only had a few miles to cover I told myself, while also making a mental note to be sure to find a campsite or B&B before dark each night. When I closed to within a mile or so of the campsite, I kept stopping and pointing my light at any signs I passed to make sure I wasn't missing it. On and on I went, still not finding the sign I was after. Eventually I did see one of the 'AA Approved' signs to the side of the road, the type you often see near campsites, but there didn't appear to be any other signs, and the little lane just looked like a farmers track. Hmm. Carrying on for a few hundred metres I couldn't see anything else more promising in the distance, and the road started dropping downhill pretty steeply, I really didn't want to drop down that only to have to turn around and come back up. I turned around and headed back to the lane, must be it surely. The lane was uneven and muddy so I got off and pushed, really didn't fancy falling off in the dark before I'd started. I was relieved to see a campsite sign a little further down, and beyond that a large empty field, except for 2 campervans nestled in the far corner and a small series of buildings off to my right. The buildings seemed to be giving off the only source of light for miles around so I gingerly headed towards them. Finding a handy section of fence nearby allowed me somewhere to lean the bike while it was unloaded. First thing to come off was my tent, which was held onto the top of my panniers with a couple of bungee cords, they held it firm and I reasoned that they could prove useful as a bodge repair item later on if needs be. With the tent off I unzipped its bag, removed the tent itself, undid the clasp which holds the tent in its disc shape, and threw it up in the air. I marvelled as it landed as a perfectly assembled tent, same as ever. I've had that tent for years now and it never ceases to amaze me with how well it works. It's stood up to all sorts of weather too and never leaked a drop, even the inner tent is suspended from the outer and falls into place on its own. It's perfect, seriously go and buy one now, then watch a Youtube video on how to repack it as yes it's very quick and easy once you know how to do it, but if you don't know how to do it! Well then it's impossible, and it does take some time before you get used to bending the poles to repack it, but that's how it's made to be used and mine is still in perfect condition after over 40 uses. Right, sales 'pitch' over, can you believe they didn't even pay me to say that! (But if you'd like to send me a little something Quechua…..)

With the tent up I opened my back right pannier which contained my sleeping bags and mat. I threw the bags into the tent and went back in for the mat. Hmm, nothing there. By now I was using the LED on my phone as a torch (rather effective it was too) but as it shone into the pannier I couldn't see the little sleeping mat anywhere. That was a bit of a worry, but surely it must be somewhere? I went through the other rear pannier, chucking extra clothes into the tent as well as things I'd need for the morning like toothpaste, toothbrush, cream, drink etc. Still no sleeping mat. The front panniers were looked through rather more in hope than expectation. The left pannier held all my bikes spares. No mat. My last hope was the right pannier which was reserved for food and my cooking supplies. Again, no sleeping mat to be found. I shone the torch around the floor, desperately hoping that I'd dropped the mat somewhere, it was only a little thing. I'd borrowed it off Uncle Bob and tried it a few weeks previously, it was surprisingly comfortable and packed much smaller than my own version so I'd decided to use it, but apparently it hadn't been packed! I resigned myself to a rather more uncomfortable nights sleep than expected, and after a quick nose around the buildings to find the toilet and see what was available for the morning, I returned to the tent and attempted to get as comfortable as possible. A pillow was the other glaring oversight in my packing, but I found that a T-shirt placed over my small dry bag containing spare clothes, made a pretty convincing substitute. The long grass was also acting as a rather decent bed of sorts, so all in all I was a reasonably happy chap as I drifted off to sleep that night, thinking about the next day, and the day after, and the day after, and the day after……..

4 DAY 1, LAND'S END TO LISKEARD

I've never been very good at sleeping in. To be fair 11 years as a Postie probably haven't helped me with that, and neither did a night without my sleeping mat, of all the things to forget Ross! Giving up on sleep altogether, I emerged from my tent at around 5am. In the dark. Very dark. My scouting mission the previous night revealed a little laundry / kitchen area near the toilet block. So after using my phone as a makeshift torch once more, and packing up my tent and the rest of my stuff, I wheeled Bants the bike down to the buildings and dug out my cooking supplies. In packing up I was relieved to find that everything slotted back into the panniers in much the same way as it had at home. Making sure everything went back into the same pannier it had come out of was a good habit to get into, there would be nothing more annoying than being stuck by the side of the road, and having to empty 4 panniers because you couldn't remember where something got packed on that particular morning. No, take a little longer and keep to the system. Roughly anyway.

With my little cooker set up I added a pasta meal and water to the pan, and left that to cook while I set about untangling the bungee cord that had gotten itself wrapped around my rear wheel spindle, as I'd pushed the bike down to the building earlier. Rookie mistake, I'd forgotten the tent was held on with 3 bungees and not 2, hence the one which hadn't been secured at both ends had done a rather splendid job of tangling around the spindle, spokes, and gears, and really didn't want to come out. By the time I did work it free, my breakfast was ready and I'd already decided two things. One, I really didn't have time to mess around with cooking in the morning, and two, I'd suddenly been hit with the enormity of the challenge that lay ahead. Trying to blank that out, I ate my pasta sitting on the floor in the kitchen, leaning against the huge washing machine. I hoped all the campsites had a little room like this, it would make things much easier, there was even a kettle and toaster, charging points etc. When I'd set off on my first attempt I was carrying a large solar charger and backup battery, my plan being to set the solar panel up on the back of the bike during the day, where it would charge the backup battery. Then overnight the backup battery would be used to charge my phone, speaker, cameras and various other gadgets I had with me that time. I'd even packed a selfie stick! This attempt was very different. Realising how good the backup batteries were (at least 3 full phone charges from each) I decided to bin off the solar charger this time, reasoning that it would probably be dark and rainy in October anyway, making it largely useless or worse, flooded, and instead just carry two backup batteries and beg somewhere to charge them a few times during the trip. If all the campsites had a room like this with charging points that would be easy, I could even have gotten away with one I thought. No, better to be safe, if that phone breaks or goes flat you're properly stuffed.

As I finished breakfast with a slightly burnt mouth, as time was rapidly getting away from me, with daylight beginning to creep over the horizon, I hastily rinsed out my pan, repacked the pannier and made a final trip to the toilet before setting off. Oh, ass cream! Sorry, the chances are that if you're reading this book you're a cyclist, and hence know all about the various creams and gels we all use to keep everything 'manageable' in the downstairs area. If you're not a cyclist, then, well here's your education. Every long ride starts for every cyclist the same way, visiting a toilet and applying your chosen cream (Assos Chamois Crème being my personal choice) to the more vulnerable areas under your lycra padded shorts. The stuff is nothing short of miraculous. I won't mention it again but assume it's part of the morning routine!

With that delicate issue taken care of, I set off just after 7am, riding out of the campsite and continuing on down the road I'd been struggling to navigate in the dark a few hours earlier. It had taken me over two hours from getting up to leaving the campsite I thought to myself, that's just much too long. The cooker would have to go, plus what if it was raining and there was nowhere indoors to escape to? Thankfully this morning was dry and I'd had a little room all to myself, but I knew I wouldn't be that lucky for the whole trip. No, I needed a better faster plan. I carried on, quickly covering the remaining 5 miles, until I could see the buildings at Land's End down a hill in front of me. I'd never visited Land's End before, a strange thing as I only live in the next county, but I'd seen pictures, mostly from other cyclist's challenges, and recognised what I was seeing. The whole place is much more commercialised than John O'Groats with shops and attractions. John O'Groats is pretty much just a signpost, the odd shop and a whole lot of nothing!

As I rolled down the hill towards my start point, I surprised myself as a tear rolled down my cheek. What gives man, you're supposed to be a toughened adventurer for a few weeks now! I'm not one for crying, but I'd been thinking about how amazing it should have been to arrive here at the end of July having successfully finished the trip, and how determined I was to pull it off this time, and roll up at that sign at the very tip of Scotland in a fortnight. I gave myself a mental talking to as I passed around the entrance gate, in search of the iconic sign. The whole place was utterly deserted, not a person in sight, all the shops closed being so early on a Saturday morning. Veering off left only brought me to a hotel and a dead end, so I retraced my tracks through the shops and then saw the sign I was looking for in front of me, standing proud with the cliffs and sea behind it. Two cyclists were already there, posing for photos. We had a quick chat and they told me they were setting off on a day trip towards Devon. They kindly took a couple photos of me and 'Bants' at the sign, before we wished each other luck and they set off on their own adventure. I watched with slight jealousy as they effortlessly cycled off on their lightweight bikes, just a small pannier on the back of one of them. By contrast 'Bants' was already feeling much slower and harder work than usual. He couldn't not be of course, he was weighed down with over 20kgs of kit, which is a lot when you consider he only weighs 10kgs, plus the panniers gave it the aerodynamics of a brick. Still, aside from being a bit slower and harder work than usual, he did still feel pretty much like a bike, I just had to remember the extra width at the back end, and not to cut corners too tightly as the front panniers hung low enough to catch on kerbs. Jamming the pannier into a kerb was a sure way to make it dig in, whip the handlebars to the left and send me flying again. I had to be careful, I couldn't crash again.

After giving the other cyclists a minute or so to head off down the road, I set off. I don't normally mind riding with random cyclists, but it was the start of a big solo adventure, and it felt right to set off on my own. Giving 'Bants' a little pat, I promised to look after him if he looked after me, and set off. Past the shops, the entrance, past the painted 'Start' signs and along the road I'd just travelled down, heading back towards the campsite, back towards Penzance in fact. The first 12 miles or so would thus be familiar to me, having already travelled them in the opposite direction, the down side to this was I knew in advance just how many hills there were in those 12 miles! I did briefly think before I left, that it would be quite cool to say I'd done the whole thing without having to get off and push once…but that was wildly optimistic. I was pushing, and I was pushing within the first half hour. With hindsight I should probably have changed the gearing on the bike before leaving, it's fine for lightweight Sunday Sportives, but loaded up with a load of kit on a long tour? No, massively over geared, like trying to drive everywhere in your car without 1st or 2nd gear. On the plus side I reasoned that as I was expecting to be 'on the move' for up to 10 hours a day, then a little break from sitting on the saddle would be a welcome relief. In truth this was my biggest worry, spending that long on the saddle after being off it for so long. I'd fitted one of the legendary Brooks saddles in the early summer before my first trip, many long distance cyclists swear by them and I'd decided to see what all the fuss was about. It's a real antique looking item compared to the rest of the racing saddles I'd ever used, and at first I didn't think it felt any comfier. So many people said it could take up to 500, or even 1000 miles to 'break in' the seat and mould it to your own shape though, and as I only had a couple hundred miles on it at the start of the trip I decided to stick with it. It was already as comfortable as my normal saddle, I just hoped it would get better over time.

So, with the occasional push up hill giving my rear end a break from the saddle, me and Bants pressed on, past last nights campsite and on towards Penzance. The weather was with me, staying dry and not too cold, I felt just right in my cycling shorts teamed up with a T-shirt, jumper, and cycling jacket to keep the wind off. Everything felt possible, it all felt completely doable. I stopped and sent a few texts, took a few pictures, and passed through Penzance, 12 miles or so from Land's End, and onwards, onto more unfamiliar roads.

Shortly after Penzance I stopped again, briefly, to take a couple pics of St.Michaels Mount, a place I'd heard of but had never visited before. It's basically a small tidal island just off the coast, which is linked to the town of Marazion by a man-made causeway of granite setts, passable between mid-tide and low water. I'd love to have made the trip across, and on my original attempt this is the sort of thing there would have been time for, but a couple pics would have to make do this time. I popped my phone back into its holder and carried on into Marazion, then glanced down at my phone again as a warning noise alerted me to the fact that I was off course. Stopping and turning the screen on, I attempted to see my error. This was the only slight drawback to my plan of using my phone for everything. If I left the screen on all day to display the map in front of me, then the phone would simply die within 3 or 4 hours, so my solution was to turn the screen off but leave my navigation app (called Ride with GPS) open. It already had the traffic free route loaded in, and would still plot my course along it even with the screen turned off. Unfortunately it didn't work like the sat nav in your car and call out directions to follow, but it did beep if you went off course, and I figured if I just flicked the screen on every few miles to check progress, then it shouldn't be too much of a problem to stay on track. With the screen on I zoomed in and checked for the turning I'd missed. It seems I'd only just missed it, the warning beep for being 'off course' cutting in nice and quickly. Turning around and taking the correct road, a very small road, I left the screen on for a moment as it looked like the next short part of the journey had quite a few twists and turns. I cursed as the tiny road took me over several massive hills, before having to turn off a few more times until I was on a proper single track lane. A real grass in the middle of the road affair. It was while cycling down this lane, with no turn off options, that my off course beep started going again. What? I thought to myself, there's no options here! How can I have gone wrong? Zooming right in on the map showed that the plotted route veered off from the lane I was cycling down. But where? There hadn't been any turnings. I looked at where the lane was heading and saw that it was in a completely different direction to the route I was supposed to be on. I'd have to find where I'd gone wrong. I turned around, nearly leaning the bike too far over in doing so, and only just about managing to avoid ending up on the floor, and headed back where I'd come from. To my right I saw a gate, lined up perfectly with where my route thought I should be going. No, surely not. Beyond the gate lay a path. No, that's much too kind a description. Beyond the gate lay a 3 foot wide gap between two hedgerows, a muddy, rough and rocky 3 foot wide gap. Who on earth thought this was a sensible place to be on a pushbike? I was becoming irritated as I pushed Bants through the gate and gingerly cycled down the 'path', desperately hoping that it would improve quickly. It did not. Fair enough doing the route in October wasn't helping, but this was still a terrible place to be on a road bike. I was either sinking down into the mud on my skinny wheels, or bouncing around uncontrollably on the rougher drier parts. At times the panniers were brushing both hedgerows on either side of me. Checking the map revealed that there were literally no roads near me to bail out and join into, it was either carry on or turn back and retrace my route for miles to get back to a proper road. I carried on, trying to be careful, mindful that my arm was still far from fully healed, that the bike was getting a right bashing and still had to do the best part of 1200 miles, that the panniers were jumping around all over the place. But I was getting severely wound up at being here. This carried on for far too long before unbelievably the path opened out into what appeared to be some sort of abandoned quarry. It was certainly rough enough to be. I'd lost my temper by this point. "Who on earth would come up with this as a route for a long distance cycle tour!" More bumps, surely me and the bike couldn't take this. What if this mad man had planned the whole route like this? "Pathetic!" I shouted to the empty surroundings, as I got smashed from pillar to post trying to make my way through the boulders covering the path.

Further on and I'd just given up being careful, deciding that speed was the answer. I was flying along, literally at times, much to the surprise of the other cyclists encountered, who were all on full suspension mountain bikes, and more than a little surprised to see some lunatic on a fully loaded road bike come bouncing past them, panniers flapping all over the show. Finally my torment was ended and I found a passable road. I got off, refastened my panniers and gave the bike a quick look over. Thankfully it seemed to have taken the punishment which was remarkable, I still had a full complement of spokes and everything else looked to be okay. Hoping no damage was hiding I carried on, never being so thankful for a bit of smooth tarmac.

Realising I hadn't eaten since breakfast, I stopped at Portreath and had a couple of bacon sarnies as I looked out to sea. It was a stunning little beach and I don't know if it was the hunger or the setting, but they were the finest bacon sandwiches I've ever had. Very nearly went back for a third but I'd gotten strange enough looks asking for two in the first place! Glancing at the time as I left Portreath, I realised it was nearly midday. I really needed to crack on. I had to cover 100 miles a day if I wanted to keep my 2 days in reserve, in case I had any bike related disasters or just needed a rest day. 100 miles a day. 160kms. No that sounds much worse, 100 miles a day then. I worried that this would be an unachievable target, especially on the silly tracks this route was taking me down. I hoped that had been the only dodgy part of the route, that somehow I'd found the one bad bit in the first morning, and that now everything would be okay. Idiot. Optimistic idiot.

The route continued to give me problems. At one point I was on a perfectly quiet wide road, when my route sent me across the road, over a small bridge and down a path the other side of a field. I continued on this path for maybe half a mile before cycling back to the road I had been on and continuing. This was a joke. I'm all for avoiding busy roads but how much time had I just wasted, firstly going over there to cycle half a mile on a little path, and also stopping to check my map, when the original road was deserted anyway? I made the decision there and then to bin off this route, there was just no way to make it all the way to Scotland in two weeks like this. This did of course give me some problems and bad news, but also good news.

Pros of binning off the route –

I could almost certainly go a more direct route. Less miles is a good thing.

I can use real roads, and as such I'm far less likely to break the bike, or just fall off trying to cycle somewhere not really suitable for a road bike.

I hopefully won't have to keep stopping and checking my map every 5 seconds, as I'm likely to stay on roads for longer. I can just aim for big towns along my route instead of constantly jumping from roads to lanes to bridleways, cycle paths, canal paths etc.

I might not go and strangle the man who devised this route.

Cons of binning off the route –

If I'd known in advance I'd have planned a route in advance. I'd have checked out roads on Google Street View where necessary, I'd have avoided the major ones. Okay I know the worst roads in Devon and Cornwall, but past that I'll be winging it a bit.

It's another job to be done on the way. Or at night for the next day.

There's nobody to blame if I end up lost! ;)

In the end it was an easy decision to go my own way, I really didn't see that there was much choice anyway. I left the original route programmed into my phone to use as a reference, but zoomed out and had a quick look at the rough direction I wanted to be heading in. If I kept to my 100 miles a day on the original route, that should leave me somewhere near Plymouth by the end of day one. Looking at the map I saw no reason why I needed to go anywhere near Plymouth at all. I was currently just outside Truro and decided to stick to the A390, which would take me just south of St.Austell and on towards Liskeard. Mum and Dad were planning on meeting me at the end of day one to relieve me of all my cooking supplies (I really didn't want to throw away Uncle Bobs camping stove and pan sets, as well as my stuff) so I sent Mum a few hasty texts explaining that I wouldn't be near Plymouth as planned, but instead somewhere else. Details to follow when I knew!

Progress was much easier and direct on my new roads, but I still had a bit to learn about navigating on the way and kept checking my progress a little too often, which slowed me more as I worried about heading in the wrong direction. The weather also decided to get in on the act and really began to give me a kicking as the afternoon wore on. I pulled out my ace card, a bag for my phone which had been made for divers etc to take their phones underwater! I figured if it could handle that it could definitely handle some rain on a pushbike, the only downside was that in its very waterproof bag the phone no longer fitted in the handlebar holder, so instead I had to store it in the little bag I'd fastened to my top tube. This meant stopping and getting the phone out of the bag every time I needed to check directions, which was a little annoying, although it did make me press on a bit more. Also in the top tube bag for easy access, were my small bike lock, so I could at least secure the bike a little when popping into shops, my Go Pro camera, and a little Ziploc freezer bag with my debit card and some cash. I promised myself that I'd never go anywhere without both my phone and debit card. Even if everything else got stolen, at least I could sort something out with a phone and some money. Without those as well it would be an even bigger problem!

With the rain worsening I finally gave in and put my waterproof jacket back on, although I'd left it too late and with my jumper already wet it wasn't long before I was feeling cold. I passed St.Austell sometime after 3pm, feeling knackered, cold, soaked through and absolutely terrible. I had a quick look at my route and decided I had to get as far as Liskeard, another 20 miles or so. As I was cold and soaking I also wanted a warm bed, and Liskeard had a Premier Inn so that would do nicely, so after sending a quick text to the parents telling them where I planned on being, I carried on.

The following 20 miles were without doubt the most miserable I've ever completed on a bike. I realised, much too late, that I hadn't eaten enough, and rather annoyingly I couldn't find any shops or garages. There was an immense amount of food with me in my panniers but it all required cooking, and I couldn't really do that by the roadside in the pouring rain. I just wanted something, anything, that I could stuff right now. Freezing cold, exhausted, very wobbly, and starting to have problems focusing. This was terrible, like I was in trouble and needed saving, what on earth was I doing here? Why? Because you don't like losing Ross. Now get on with it. So on and on I struggled, until eventually coming across a little garage, brief shelter from the cold and rain as well as a massive hot pasty, large mars bar and a twix. Not healthy but just what was needed and I felt so much better for it. This was a real lesson in how important it was going to be to keep myself fed properly, and I promised myself that I would keep one pannier on the bike full up with food from day two onwards. Food I could just reach in, unwrap and eat, there couldn't be another repeat of this.

With some food in my stomach the last few miles into Liskeard were covered much easier, still being freezing cold and soaked wet through but at least I felt like me again, not like I was about to collapse at the roadside. As I entered the town I switched from my cycling navigation app to Google maps to find the Premier Inn. Again I selected the cycle option and again got myself lost, as the app seemed intent on sending me down into a carpark with no path through the other side of it that I could see. I cursed Google for the second day in succession, and looked at the map myself before picking my own route to that nights bed. Oh how I was looking forward to a nice warm bed.

Mum text to say they'd arrived in Liskeard and were just driving to the Premier Inn, perfect timing, we literally turned up at the roundabout next to it at the same time. As they had the campervan, I jumped in and dried off a little before grabbing all my cooking supplies off the bike, and leaving them in the camper. I then refilled the pannier with a load of supplies from the camper, and grabbed my spare sleeping mat which happened to still be in there, thankyou parents! With that taken care of, I headed over to the Premier Inn only to find out it was full! Full! Why on earth were they fully booked at 6:30pm on a Saturday night in Cornwall? What was anyone doing here? Bugger. I trudged back to the camper unsure of what to do next. Liskeard is a reasonable size place I thought, there must be a B&B or something here surely?

In the end my arm was twisted and with home less than 50 miles away, my very insistent parents drove me back there for the night. I could live with that. So long as I was dry and warm that was good. But did I want to come back and start again the next day? That was the question. I didn't know. I really didn't want to fail again, to let myself and other people down, but I also felt like death that afternoon and didn't think I had another few weeks in me like that. And it was October after all, it could rain the whole trip, what would I do in the remote parts of Scotland? Where there might not be a B&B or hotel for miles? I couldn't imagine getting into a tent in this weather, at the end of a long day, already freezing cold and soaked. And presumably in over 1000 miles time I'd be in a bit of a mess anyway. What do I do? I went rather quiet as I normally do when I'm worried about something. The parents weighed in with their views, my phone buzzed with a few more. I don't know. Yes I do, I do know. If I quit now I have to go home and kick myself for the next two weeks. And I won't let everyone down again. I will do this.

Distance Travelled – 87 Miles
Hedgerows watered – 2
Pasties Eaten – 1
Time shouted at Google Maps - 2
Times nearly given up – 17

5 DAY 2, LISKEARD TO TAUNTON

It felt slightly odd to be waking up at my parents house on day two of the trip, certainly not part of the plan, but then this whole trip was going to be about improvising and changing plans on the way. I was relieved to find that once up and out of bed I felt okay, a bit of a cold and cough but nothing major, pleasingly there didn't seem to be any particularly bad aches or pains from the previous day. My dodgy arm also seemed to be okay, right then, reasons to be cheerful! We all piled into the camper by 6am for the trip back to Liskeard, and at just after 7am I was jumping on the bike and resuming my adventure from that same roundabout where I'd nearly thrown in the towel the previous night. Well I did throw in the towel actually, I'd just dried myself off with it and it was soaking!

With the weather looking dodgy I was determined not to make the same mistake I'd made on day one. There would be no more 'get out of jail free cards' on this trip, I needed to make sure to do my absolute best to avoid getting to the point where I was so cold and wet that I couldn't help myself. As a result the day began with me wearing jog bottoms and waterproof trousers over my lycra shorts, as well as a jumper and waterproof jacket over my T-shirt. I expected it to be too many layers for later on in the day, but for first thing it was perfect. As well as sorting out my clothing on the journey down, I'd also been studying the maps on my phone to figure out where I'd be heading throughout the day, a task made admittedly slightly easier by living locally to the area. I'd managed 87 miles on the first day when I was aiming for 100, my more direct route though had made up for the difference so I figured was still on target. Comparing the route I now planned on taking on day two, versus the original planned route would also save me a fair chunk of distance. I was hoping to get ahead of schedule during the next couple days as my route looked more direct up until the midland's area, when they would be reasonably close mileage wise. Then looking further ahead it appeared I could save a chunk more mileage in Scotland....but that seemed like a scary long way ahead to be looking! I zoomed back in on southern England and promised myself I would not look that far ahead again, I had to keep tackling this in very small steps if I was going to win. Deal with one problem and move on. Solve the problem after that. Then the next and the next. I could see many problems that would arise before the finish in Scotland, and many more which I was sure would catch me by surprise, but I just kept telling myself that if I solved enough problems then eventually I would win. And that's the mind-set I carried with me as I set off from Liskeard on day two.

Finding my way out of town, I continued on following the A390 from the previous day. Being the south west there were of course many hills to contend with, pretty soon I did have to stop to remove my jog bottoms and jumper, but did keep my waterproofs on to protect me from the intermittent rain and wind. That felt immediately better once moving again. I knew the first 'big place' I was aiming for on day two was Tavistock, nearly 20 miles from Liskeard. Distances like this seemed like a good way to break up the day, rather than looking at it as one big chunk. Just cycle to Tavistock, simple enough. What wasn't simple were the hills, as the quiet road twisted and turned its way up and down, Gunnislake and Gulworthy being particular early morning tests of climbing and descents. Strangely it was the descents which were causing me unexpected problems, as I was finding it difficult to squeeze the back brake lever very much with my left arm. I settled for gentle braking on that rear brake, with most of the effort going through my right arm and the front brake. It seemed to work for the most part but I was glad I'd fitted some soft grippy brake blocks for the trip.

Half past nine and I found myself back 'home' in Devon and rolling through Tavistock. I was pleased, this had been a good start to the day. Also pleasing was my new 'food pannier' which was keeping my energy levels and good mood topped up! Already there had been a couple occasions when I'd been pushing up a hill, and found myself reaching into the 'pannier of plenty' for a little snack. Best decision of the trip so far. Easily.

With Tavistock down I carried on, with the weather and my mood ever improving. The next target so to speak was Okehampton, which would be met after a trip up the west side of Dartmoor on the A386. This was as close to my house on the other side of Dartmoor that I would get, from this point on I would be travelling away from home. This being Dartmoor there were of course more than a couple hills, but they were to be expected and progress was still good, arriving in Okehampton around midday. I felt much happier and more confident than on day one, and was actually looking forward to getting further north, to more unfamiliar places. As I said earlier I'm a bit of a strange person and not terribly confident, although my friend will always say this is absolute rubbish and that I'm the most confident person in the world. Not at all true. We normally agree to disagree on that one…..even though I'm right. But this whole trip, and the last few years of my life really, have been about me doing things out of my comfort zone, and I was surprised to find myself actually looking forward to some of the challenges ahead and all the unknowns with it. Like where would I be staying tonight for instance? Where would I be eating? What roads would I use tomorrow? The day after? What would I do if I badly broke the bike? No idea, no idea whatsoever to any of it, and I was thrilled to find that didn't scare me completely silly, it excited me.

Past Okehampton and onto some stunning cycling roads, quiet wide deserted roads with just the occasional tractor for company, perfect. The weather was now also dry and looking like staying that way for the rest of the day, I was feeling generally very chuffed with myself and my navigation, as I sped through Bow and Copplestone. Glancing at the map, I decided to use a few small 'white roads' shown to straight line my route a little and skirt north of Crediton, such was my newfound confidence. This was a mistake. The roads really were small and so steep I had to resort to pushing. I expect the main road, although slightly longer, would have been much flatter and faster…and it's not like it looked like it was a particularly dangerous busy road, I was just getting a little too eager to straighten my route out. As it was I emerged from my 'short cut' (which included one hilarious farm track that I had to push the bike through) out onto the main road having probably wasted a good half an hour. Still, progress had generally been good and I had stopped to fix an issue that had been developing with my front panniers.

When the front panniers had arrived they're seemed slightly thin and a little flimsy, but it was getting close to me setting off for Land's End and I'd run out of time to find a better alternative. They'd kept their shape okay on day one but had seemed to start sagging more throughout the second day, plus I hadn't helped matters by removing the solid boxes containing my tea / sugar / cooker, and replacing them with lots of individually wrapped cereal bars etc. Whereas the boxes helped the panniers keep their shape, lots of small items just all dropped to the bottom of the bag, trying to drag it into the front wheel. Not good. The bumpy 'short cut' had really highlighted a serious problem, so I did the sensible thing and stopped to try and bodge a repair. Fortunately a background in motorsport teaches you how to bodge most things, so armed with everyones favourite items, cable ties and tank tape, I soon had the panniers secured well away from my wheel and potential disaster!

Back onto a decent, but still rather hilly Devon road (the A3072) I carried on into Tiverton. Arriving at around 3:30pm, my reward for passing the 100km mark (62 miles) for the day, was to grab an armful of food from a garage and stuff a great deal of it, before restocking the pannier of plenty with the rest. Feeling fuller and ready to go again, I checked the map and decided that if I braved the 'Devon Expressway' for a couple miles, a whole lot of messing around on small 'white roads' could be saved, and I'd be back on a sensible road to head towards Taunton. I'm not sure why I made that decision really. I remember being in a bit of a rush and thinking that although it was a dual carriageway, there would be a shoulder to cycle in, that it was only a couple miles, and that it was a Sunday afternoon, how busy would it be? All utter rubbish and one of the worst decisions by far. As soon as I got on that road I knew it was a terrible idea. My one saving grace was that the wind had picked up and was blowing me along at a solid 15 – 20mph, sometimes more, so I wouldn't be on the road for more than a few minutes. But it was still not a good place to be, even on the shoulder. I'd never concentrated so much to keep speed up and to keep over as far as possible without having any wobbles. Must be half way there I thought, legs burning from keeping up the pace, before suddenly there was a loud clang and I slowed. Puncture. Immediate very large puncture. Fortunately I was right at the start of a layby, so there was plenty of room to pull the bike over out of harms way and get to work. My organised pannier system worked a treat, as I quickly dived into the correct pannier and produced a spare inner tube, tyre levers and pump. With that out I flipped the bike over, not the easiest of tasks when it's as heavy and bulky as it now was, and unclipped the rear panniers so they dropped out of the way and allowed me a bit more access to the rear wheel. Normally changing tyres and tubes on modern bikes is very quick and easy, but all these extras strapped to the bike were certainly making it slightly more interesting. Undoing the quick release skewer I whipped the wheel out, pulled the tyre off the rim and removed the punctured tube. That got thrown into a bag to investigate later, no time for that now, I wanted out of here. A quick look at the rim and tyre was next to make sure there were no issues there, nothing still stuck in the tyre that would immediately puncture my new inner tube. Nope, it all looked good so the new tube and the tyre were mounted, inflated and dropped back into the bike before flipping it back over. Levers and pump were thrown into the pannier and I was out of there in record time! I did not want to spend any longer on that road than absolutely necessary. A few minutes later (and according to the data after topping 25mph!) I was off the 'death road', back onto a much more suitable one and telling myself I was an idiot. I'd promised people I would be careful, yet I'd ended up on a stupid road just because I didn't want to mess around diverting through some lanes. I promised myself I would not make that error again.

It felt good to be back on a safe road as me and Bants began to creep a few miles closer towards our next target of Taunton. Just as I was thinking I would stop at the next campsite, I had that familiar feeling from the bike I'd had a mere 10 miles earlier, puncture! No! I thought to myself, pulling over and again going through the same process I'd just completed. I didn't understand what was going on, I always run good Continental Tyres and inner tubes, and as a result just don't get punctures….until now. As I worked away, mindful of the time ticking on, I decided that I must have accidentally pinched a bit of the inner tube between the edge of the rim and the tyre, in my rush to change the first flat and get off the dual carriageway. Yes that must be it. I rang Dad as I refitted the wheel and he had the same thought. With the parents on the phone I also asked if they could log into my Wiggle account (the cyclists go to online shop) and order me some extra inner tubes and a tyre to be sent to my auntie and uncles house in Evesham, where I planned to be in a couple days time. I'd only brought three spare inner tubes with me and I'd now used two of them in very short succession, it made me feel very vulnerable as I cycled off with just the one spare tube remaining.

Continuing on and trying to forget about my tyre troubles, I thought I'd better head towards the next campsite I saw as it was nearly 5pm….except I didn't want to. All of a sudden I seemed to have cleared the worst of Cornwall and Devon's relentless hills, the roads were gently rolling, the wind was behind me, the weather was good and I was flying along. Okay, I thought to myself, I feel reasonably comfortable on the bike and who knows how bad the weather might be tomorrow, just keep going and bank the miles now while the weathers good. If you leave this until tomorrow you could end up cycling this road in the rain, into a massive headwind, who knows what. Keep going now instead, keep going while the going's good!

So that's what I did, revelling in the perfect conditions I breezed into Taunton at just gone 6pm, where my good mood was smacked right out of me as I again picked up a puncture, while making my way through the middle of town. I bumped up onto the wide pavement outside a Tesco and asked myself what on earth was going on. 3 punctures! 3! In one day! This made no sense at all, I hadn't had 3 punctures in the previous 3 years, let alone in one day. Again the bike was whipped over and the tube replaced. This was it, my last spare. I spent a good five minutes examining my tyre and rim for any problems, however slight, but there just weren't any. In a fit of despair that this problem would keep happening I rang Dad for advice, and to moan a little, because it's just not the same if there's no one around to hear you moan. Dad had a theory. Of course he did, Dad always had a theory. I listened as he explained what was happening, then examined my punctured tubes for evidence. Yes, I thought, he was right.

Basically the problem was coming from not having enough air in the tyre. When I'm at home I use my big high capacity 'track pump' to inflate the tyres, and would normally pressure to around 80psi. This is what I'd run all year and had been the pressures set when I left home a few days earlier. The problem came when I got my first puncture, this had likely been a normal puncture, picked up by running over debris, but when it came to inflating my new tube I only had my small lightweight mini pump with me. Now, it's a great bit of kit and packs up nice and small, but it just wasn't possible to get the same pressure using it as I would at home with my big pump. Couple the lower tyre pressure with the fact that Bants had a lot more weight on him than usual, mix in some of England's many potholes and this was my problem. When the tyre, with its lower pressure, hit a particularly bad hole, the weight of me and the bike effectively squashed it too much, resulting in the inner tube being 'pinched' and giving me the punctures. Staring at my old tubes under the worsening light, revealed the most recent two of them to each have two small holes in them, right alongside each other on both edges of the tube. Right then, thanks Dad, theory definitely confirmed. I squeezed every last bit of air possible into my final tube, to the point where I thought I was either going to break my pump or my arm, but fortunately they both took the punishment. I did now have a bit of a dilemma though with no more new tubes on me. There was a Halfords in Taunton but they'd already closed for the day and wouldn't be reopening until 9am the next day. Ideally I wanted to crack on now and find a campsite outside of town and be well on my way north long before 9am, not coming back into town and waiting around for a shop to open. Decisions decisions. I dithered for a few seconds, ready to go but not sure what to do for the best. I was fairly confident I'd have less problems now the cause of the punctures was clear, plus there were a few puncture repair patches in my spares. I reasoned I'd head to a campsite now, and once there patch my 3 punctured tubes in case I got any more punctures before arriving at my auntie and uncles in Evesham, and could collect my new ones. I'm never particularly keen on running on repaired tubes, but I knew it wasn't going to be for the duration of the trip and I really didn't want to be wasting several hours the next morning. I needed to keep moving forwards! Progress!

With some air in my tyres and the wind still with me, I was happy to escape the town and even happier to spot a sign for a campsite a few miles further down the road. Even though it was nearing 7pm I was astounded to find that I still didn't really want to stop, sure my rear end felt a little bit uncomfortable at times but nothing too bad, no worse than a normal Sunday ride really, and the rest of me felt in pretty good condition to. Still, it would be getting dark soon, and after my night-time adventures in Cornwall I was keen to find somewhere to stay before a repeat of that fun! Following the camping signs I turned off the main road at Monkton Heathfield and rolled through a new housing estate, all the time wondering where a campsite could be hiding amongst all these new homes. I did have a brief worry that perhaps the houses had been built over the campsite, but soon enough the road looped around and presented me with Tanpits Farm Campsite to finish day two. Being a farm I soon found someone in the main house to book me in and point me in the direction of the small field. Picking a quiet corner beside the stables I threw my tent up, a job made much easier than on my first night thanks to the last of the remaining daylight. With my bed for the night ready, Bants was secured to the fence alongside my tent and I went for a shower. Oh how nice a hot shower felt after 12 hours on a bike! 12 hours I thought to myself. Wow. I'd never spent anywhere near that amount of time on a bike in one day before. In fact I'd only spent half that time in the saddle before. I made my way back to the tent feeling rather pleased with myself and quite honestly surprised. My mood and my belief that I could maybe manage to finish this challenge were both massively improved over where they'd been the previous day. I knew there would be lots of challenges and rough days ahead, but as I zipped myself up in my tent, sent some excited text messages, and stuffed my face with immense amounts of food from my panniers, I thought for the first time that yes, I might actually be able to do this.

Distance Travelled – 93 Miles
Hedgerows watered – 1 (3 Total)
Punctures – 3

Campsite – 7/10. Fair price, nice chap, smart clean toilet and showers. Small farm setting. (Possibly rising to 10/10 if you like your farm cider as they make it!)

6 DAY 3, TAUNTON TO EVESHAM

After a good nights sleep on my mat I was up bright and early to start day three, and delighted to peer out of my tent and find blue skies. I really didn't relish the thought of trying to pack everything up in the rain, so to start the day dry was always a massively pleasing thing. All packed up and again having had a small 'breakfast' courtesy of my panniers, I topped up my water bottles and set off. Finding my way back through the housing estate and onto the main road was easy enough, but once there I just couldn't seem to get comfortable. My back had ached a little when I'd gotten out of bed but that felt okay now. My rear felt slightly uncomfortable though as I moved around on the saddle, unable to get anywhere near as happy with my position as I had been at the end of the previous day. My legs were aching too. Hmm. This wasn't the start of the day I was looking for.

Five miles in and my bleary eyes spotted a burger

van in a layby on the opposite side of the road. Well, it's not like I'd had a proper breakfast was it? After waiting an age for a gap in the traffic, I crossed over and ordered the biggest and most calorie filled thing on the chalkboard menu, a large bacon, double egg, double sausage baguette. Plus for good measure, and while the owner was giving me his life story as he cooked my breakfast, I downed a cup of tea and a large cake. Never mind all the professional energy bars and gels, this is how I would power myself for my trip! The BBC filmed an amazing program years ago which followed Eddie Izzard as he completed 43 marathons in 51 days, a simply stunning achievement, especially seeing his complete lack of meaningful preparation. It also seems he'd managed to sustain himself, in large parts at least, through alcohol and ice cream. Well I'm not a big drinker, but I could still learn from the man and didn't fear a bit of junk food for the duration of my trip! Now, if you haven't already seen the brilliant Eddie Izzard documentary, 'Marathon Man' then go and watch it. For some ridiculous reason it's not available on DVD but go and search Youtube, it'll be there somewhere and it's compelling viewing.

Back to the morning of day three and I greedily tucked into my naughty breakfast, as my newest roadside friend finished bringing me up to date with his life up until that point. Cliff notes version – long distance lorry driver for Argos for many years, left, decided to run his own burger van. A very good burger van it was too as we discussed what had happened to the 'Wimpys' fast food chain in recent years. "I used to love those" he said. "There's one in Newton Abbot near where I live for some reason I noticed the other day, apparently it's only one of a few left. No idea why, it's almost like they forgot to close it!" I told him as I continued to stuff my face, this had definitely been a good decision. "Oh I know it well, used to go there when I was in the area with Argos. Still there?" "Still there." I finished my breakfast and headed off, wondering if the burger van might be shutting behind me and heading off to Newton Abbot, in search of a dodgy fast food restaurant and a nostalgic memory.

Back in the saddle and after a few miles I began to feel more comfortable, which soon wiped out any guilt over stopping so early. I stuck to the A38 which was reasonably quiet and wide enough to not be causing me any concerns. Plus as I continued north, through Bridgewater, the M5 was never far away, so most of the traffic would instead be heading onto the motorway in preference to the smaller roads. On and on I travelled, feeling better and better as the morning wore on, and being massively relieved to find this! Just gone 11am and I was passing Bristol Airport and starting to worry about having to navigate the first real city of my trip, Bristol.

My original planned route (the one I'd binned off on day one) would have me ploughing right through Bristol city centre. I didn't see the reason for this but accepted that it wasn't possible to avoid it altogether, there just weren't the roads available to do it without resorting to massively time consuming detours, on tiny roads. I did have a compromise though, and I was very thankful for the dry day which allowed me to leave my phone on the handlebars, with my map and current location displayed as I tried to follow the plan I'd come up with sat in my tent the previous night. Continuing on the A370 until just south of Bristol, I then joined the A369 which snuck me up the west side of Bristol alongside the River Avon. A little residential road then took me right up to the impressive Clifton Suspension Bridge. Well that had been easy! After crossing the bridge I decided I couldn't pass such a big landmark without grabbing a photo, so I turned back and leant Bants against the side of the bridge for a few snaps. Checking my map again I now just had to zig zag my way through a few residential streets and out through Clifton, Henleaze, and finally Filton, before emerging back out into the countryside. Easy! With it now lunchtime and feeling happy with progress, and having some more confidence in my ability to navigate my way around, I stopped at a chipshop for lunch. Good decision. If you're ever in the area then I thoroughly recommend Henleaze Fish Bar, certainly put a smile on my face!

As I waited to be served I noticed Bants had drawn some attention outside. This was becoming a bit of a familiar sight, as people seemed to have to find out where I was heading on a bike loaded up with so much gear. Often a fellow cyclist would seem to appear out of nowhere, knowingly eyeing up the bike and realising where I was heading. It astounded me just how many people approached saying they'd completed the trip before, or their Dad / partner / friend etc had. It seems there's lots of lunatics on our little island!

Feeling happy and well fed I continued on my way, putting Bristol behind me and revelling in the slight tail wind that was making my day so much easier. If you're not a cyclist I cannot tell you how much difference a bit of wind can make. For the same amount of effort on your part, you can either be struggling along at walking pace on the flat into a headwind, or barreling along the same piece of road with great speed. Plus if you are making good progress you're naturally feeling happier, more capable, and more energetic, whereas when you're struggling into the wind and getting nowhere, you wear yourself out, make painfully slow progress and generally feel pretty rubbish and downbeat. Wind then, makes a big difference.

With the wind behind me I breezed onwards up the A38 for nearly 30 miles until reaching Gloucester. That had without doubt been the easiest piece of cycling of the trip. I made a mental note to do more cycling outside of Devon and Cornwall and away from their notorious hills. I pulled over into a layby just before Gloucester and plotted my route through, and onwards towards my uncles just outside Evesham. Hmm, how far away was Evesham now? I zoomed out a little and did a bit of quick math. Probably around 30 miles, and it was only around 4pm. That's manageable, I thought to myself. Plus, if I were to stop so close to them tomorrow I wouldn't be able to stay. I couldn't arrive at 10am and then waste a whole day, I just didn't have the days spare for that. No, if I was this close I had to get there on day three, it's just the only way it would work.

With a target in mind, (love a target, I need to be aiming for something, always have, always will) I re-attached my phone, quickly downed a king size mars bar and set off through Gloucester like it was the start of a race. I was the stereotypical cyclist, squeezing my way past the stationary cars to the front of the queue at traffic lights, then tutting at them being red before darting off again. It's amazing how quickly you can progress through a town on a bike, and I was soon out the other side of Gloucester and pushing on up the A38 towards Tewksbury. The problem was the closer to Tewksbury I was getting, the more the wind was giving up on me. Whereas it had been straight into my back for the previous few hours, it was now blowing more across me from west to east as I headed north. Progress slowed a little and I began to worry that I'd lose the light before reaching my destination. My other worry was the road I would be taking from Tewksbury to Evesham, the A46. It was now rush hour and I knew this road would likely be quite busy, but I really didn't have many other options. On the positive side I would be travelling from west to east, so as soon as I changed roads I picked up my wonderful tail wind and really got moving again! This was a good thing as the road, as predicted, was fairly busy and not an ideal place to be cycling. With this in mind it was helpful to be able to keep up some real speed and be slightly less of a roadblock / liability. That said it's still not fun being on a busy road. Really really not fun. You can hear the cars, or worse, lorries behind you, but you never know what sort of person is driving them. For the most part drivers are kind and considerate to cyclists, but even if only 1 in every 100 isn't, then it makes you wary of the other 99. Plus of course if it's a busy day, or you happen to be cycling for several weeks on end, you are going to meet a few of those '1 in 99's'. I grimaced as a lorry came past me reasonably closely with a fair difference in speed. The road was straight but had temporarily narrowed to the point where there was no room for me and two directions of traffic to pass at the same time. The driver had seen there was a gap in the oncoming traffic and obviously timed his run on me to overtake in this gap. But he did do it quite closely, close enough for the awful aerodynamics of a lorry to do their favourite trick and quite literally try to suck you and the bike under as they go past. It's a very strange and very unpleasant feeling, the effect seeming to be heightened by the panniers fitted to the front and back of the bike. As I grimaced and held the handlebars firm, the lorry continued on by as I remained upright and intact, putting a little extra effort into my pedal strokes to get myself out of this mess. I'd promised to come back from this trip in one piece and I fully intended to keep that promise.

Several miles on and mercifully the road had widened out significantly, almost to the point where it could have been a dual carriageway. Fantastic. It was nearly 6pm and I was almost there, just a couple miles south of Evesham and at the point where I would follow the bypass for a mile or two around the outskirts, before veering off for the final mile or so to my bed for the night in Badsey. Perfect I thought to myself, what a good day, great distance, I feel great, no problems and I've got a nice warm bed and some family a few miles away. The road again narrowed on the approach to a roundabout and left me no choice but to squeeze up against the kerb, as another lorry came past. I saw a massive pothole in front of me but it was too late, I couldn't do anything to avoid it. The kerb was too steep to mount on my left, 38 tonnes of articulated lorry seemed fairly immovable to my right, and there was no way to stop in time. Bang! Followed almost instantly by Psssshhh, and a horrible sound as my wheel rim scraped along the road, no longer wrapped in its inflated tube and tyre. I admit I did sigh. I thought about pushing the bike the remaining distance but it was a little too far for that. No, there was only one thing to be done, so once again the bike got flipped over, the wheel was removed, the tyre and tube separated. I took out one of the tubes I'd repaired the night before, the one I had most hope for, and fitted it. Gingerly I re-inflated the tube, all the time waiting for my patch to be dislodged and the tyre to go down, but it seemed to be holding. With only a few miles to go I didn't go too mad with the pressure before setting off again, being very careful to avoid as many bumps and holes as possible.

6:30pm and with the daylight starting to escape I pushed Bants through my auntie and uncles garden and into the conservatory. What a day! I almost couldn't believe I was here, it was just crazy to think that in the morning I'd been in Taunton, and now here I was just outside Evesham for dinner. Bristol and the

Clifton bridge from this morning had felt like another day entirely. Very strange. After doing the maths and checking routes later on I found that I'd covered over 100 miles. I was delighted. 100 miles in a day is a bit of a rite of passage for cyclists and I'd never done it before, never really had the reason or inclination to, but to do it on this trip carrying all my gear and after such a complete lack of any training or preparation, was amazing. I was definitely ahead of schedule now and I was so going to do this.

After we'd all said our hellos and my uncle had shocked himself at the weight of the bike, we sat down for dinner, dessert and a catch-up. Perfect. My cousin Justin even popped in to say hello. Justin had joined me on a previous daft adventure a few years previously, when we'd completed the three peaks challenge. The challenge is to climb the three highest peaks in England, Scotland and Wales (Scaffell Pike, Ben Nevis and Snowdon) in a 24 hour period. It was a massively challenging but unforgettable experience, as we'd started at Ben Nevis in Scotland in the early hours of the morning, before travelling down to the Lake District and completing the gruelling Scaffell Pike climb as darkness fell, before finally reaching the top of Snowdon in the early hours of the following morning. Complete exhaustion had set in by this point, to the point where we'd managed to get lost coming down the mountain and end up following completely the wrong track. By the time we realised our mistake we'd gone too far to turn back, so ended up on the wrong side of the mountain. Without a phone signal we'd had to beg the use of a phone and then try to find a taxi (a very expensive taxi as it turned out) to get us back around the mountain to the camper van. By this point everyone was literally dead on their feet and there are some horrendous photos of us all at the finish. In fact if you flick through the photos from that weekend quick enough, I think you can actually see us all age around 5 years. I wondered if this latest adventure might have the same effect.

With Justin gone to his footy 5 a side game ("I'm going to kick people, not play football") I excused myself for a quick shower and emerged feeling much more human. It was nice to spend an evening catching up with uncle Mick and auntie Cynth, who I don't see much of due to them living a few hours away. Still, there's normally a few family events a year to drag us all together! I reclined back in my chair and decided I'd better make the most of the comfort…there wouldn't be much more of it for the next few weeks.

Distance Travelled – 106 Miles
Hedgerows watered – 2 (5 Total)
Punctures – 1 (4 Total)
Amazing Tail Winds Encountered – 1

7 DAY 4, EVESHAM TO IRONBRIDGE

I awoke the next morning feeling momentarily confused by my surroundings, before it all came back to me. I could hear my uncle downstairs and started creeping down to say morning, before remembering my auntie sleeps like the dead, at which point I carried on down the stairs without a care in the world! With my uncle off to work, I had some breakfast and gave the bike a quick glance over. Sure enough my repaired inner tube was leaking and the tyre was completely flat. No matter, my new tubes and tyres were on the way, so I stripped the old ones off the wheel in preparation. Grabbing my phone I checked the tracking info and found that they should be arriving between 11am and 12. That was okay, progress was good and a half day might not be the worst idea in the world. With the bike as ready as it could be, I started planning out my route for the next few days. It was crazy to be able to see how much the route I'd taken had differed from my planned one. The planned one even had me crossing over the bridge into Wales just after Bristol! Wildly different, and no offence to Wales but I was glad to skip it, as well as the extra mileage I've spent enough time there to know they've got hills, lots of hills!

After studying the map for a while I decided there were just too many roads to choose from, and I didn't really know any of them well enough to make a particularly informed decision. Settling on a rough plan of heading slightly north-west for a few miles to avoid Birmingham, and then as straight as possible to the north after that, pretty much as far as Scotland, is where my planning left me! I was open to revising my somewhat rough plan as the day went on though, if I found myself on any more busy roads such as on the previous day.

A few hours were spent catching up with auntie Cynth in the morning before DPD delivered my new parts just after 11am. I quickly fitted a new tube and tyre to the rear wheel and packed the rest away in my panniers, hoping they wouldn't be needed! At just gone midday I bid farewell to my auntie and thanked her for putting up a lunatic for the night, before setting off for my half day. Then I struggled. Struggled hard. The roads were busy but I'd expected that for a few miles at least, the biggest problem was the wind. This was proving doubly frustrating as I knew in my head how easy I'd been progressing the previous day, and now here I was working twice as hard to crawl along at half the speed.

After working my way back around Evesham I spent a mile or two heading north on my first choice of road, before deciding it didn't look too cyclist friendly. I checked the map and opted for a different road instead, this would take me westerly a little earlier and more abruptly than the original road, before heading through Worcester and north through the Wyre Forest. The wind might have still been fighting me a little, but I was at least now on a slightly safer road and thus feeling happier on that front.

12 miles into my half day and I stopped at a farm shop, grabbing a pasty, a large cake, and of course a copious amount of food for the pannier. (A full banana loaf indeed, can't resist those!) Sitting outside eating my lunch I kept telling myself not to be discouraged by the poor start to the day, it wasn't all going to be plain sailing, I knew that. Just keep on going, each turn of the pedals is bringing you a little bit closer to that finish line, you've just got to turn them enough times and you'll get there. Simple. I got back on the bike and turned the pedals, see, closer already.

As the afternoon wore on I passed through Worcester and then entered the Wyre Forest…and its hills. I did a lot of pushing through that forest as the afternoon turned into evening, the tall trees blocking out the light and making it feel even later than it already was. Still, it was nice to be on quieter roads again and to my relief I did eventually seem to have climbed all the hills the forest could throw at me! By this time it was gone 5pm and despite the late start I was feeling more knackered than at any other point during the trip so far. I quite fancied stopping, but there just didn't seem to be anywhere to stay. In fact the more I thought about it, I hadn't seen a single campsite all day, plus I was now in a completely deserted area, seemingly surrounded by only farms and farmhouses. Surely there must be one soon I thought to myself, as I cycled ever onwards, putting a little more effort in. It began to creep up to 6pm and I still hadn't found anywhere, couldn't even remember the last time I'd seen a pub, and they often have a room available in a pinch.

6pm, and picturing myself chucking a tent up at the side of the road, I did a little research. Well once I managed to stop somewhere my phone had data anyway. The news wasn't good as Google confirmed what I was seeing, there was just nothing. No campsites, no B&B's, nothing. At least it wasn't raining. I widened my search only to again come up with nothing. This wasn't good, it was gone 6pm and would be getting dark soon. I considered just knocking at a random farm and asking if it would be okay to pitch up somewhere, thinking people would probably take pity on a tired out looking cyclist on a mad adventure. Finally though Google did come up with an option for me, a campsite just past Ironbridge. Yes that looked like it was in vaguely the right direction too, that would do! It was slightly further away than I'd have liked given the time, but the fear of being caught out in the dark once more seemed to give my energy levels a boost as I made myself hurry on towards Ironbridge.

The sun was setting as I arrived in Ironbridge, crossing over, no surprise, a large Iron Bridge. It was a lovely little place and despite feeling very worn out and looking forward to stopping, I did make the effort to snap a few pics of the town from the bridge. I switched from my cycling navigation app to my Google maps app to find the campsite, which seemed to be on the far side of town, and annoyingly up a massive hill by the looks of it. Thinking to myself again how picturesque a place this was, this little town stretched along the River Severn, with its large amount of pubs, I continued on, then cursed as I saw the hill I still had left before I could finally call it quits for the day. No point in even trying to cycle up that. I gingerly got off the bike, lazily catching my foot on the tent secured to the top of the panniers as I swung my leg over, resulting in a quick hop on my other leg before catching my balance and trying again. Sooner or later I just knew in my tired state I was going to fall over doing that. Must be more careful. I switched my lights on, as the tree lined road was getting dark by this point as I pushed my way towards that nights finish. As the road levelled out I hopped on Bants once more as we turned into a small lane. The map was saying I'd arrived at my destination but I couldn't see anything promising around me. The lane split in two and I tried one direction for a few hundred metres before turning back and trying the other. Once around the corner on the second lane I saw the sign for Ironbridge Campsite, of course it was the second lane, if you have two choices then it'll always be the one you don't take.

The lane turned into a loose gravel affair, so I

pushed Bants up yet another hill into the campsite as the sunset treated me to a stunning orange sky overhead. Entering the site I couldn't see a reception or house anywhere. Even though it was getting late and I didn't expect to find anyone, there's still normally a note for any late arrivals left somewhere, typically something along the lines of, 'Pitch up somewhere and pay us in the morning.' But here there was nothing. At the far end of the site was a gate which looked like it led to a house, but I wasn't sure it was connected to the campsite at all, and too many years as a Postie being chased by dogs has made me wary of opening farm gates and wandering in! Thinking better of that I set the tent up in the empty field and unpacked the bike, before finding the toilet block and having a shower. With all that done and with it now completely dark, I returned to the tent and pondered my food situation. All this camping was very well, but the problem with campsites is they are invariably found in the countryside, or at least a mile or two out of town, hence no easy dinner options. I thought about all the lovely looking pubs and other places to eat which I'd cycled past a mile or two below me in the town, but it was gone 8pm, pitch black, and I was feeling properly worn out. Even with a decent light I couldn't have faced dragging my way all the way back down, and then worse, up that killer of a hill again. So, as before, I delved into my panniers for a makeshift dinner. I reasoned I'd had a decent breakfast, lunch, and been eating my normal armfuls of food in between, so was doing enough to keep my energy levels up, but I'd still have preferred a real dinner. Instead the panniers provided a banana loaf, a couple cereal bars, an apple and some sweets. Hardly a three course meal but it did the trick, as I ate with only the soft glow of my phone for company, as I updated a few people and of course, as ever, started trying to plan out the next days route. I thought, for at least the tenth time of the trip, that it really would have been nice to have all this sorted out beforehand!

With my 'dinner' eaten, and a rough idea formed of where I'd be heading the next morning, I set my alarm, and feeling like it was going to be a cold night, pulled on a second jumper before sliding into my sleeping bag, throwing another over me, pulling my hoodie up over my head and telling myself that I really must be mad to be attempting this in October.

Distance Travelled – 60 Miles
Hedgerows watered – 2 (7 Total)
Times shouted at Google Maps – 1 (3 Total)
Ridiculously cold nights – 1

Campsite – 6/10 – Decent toilet and shower block. Outside dish washing facilities are good and a small play area for children is a nice touch. Stunning views and the glamping pods looked quite cute from the outside. Marked down for being slightly awkward to find perhaps, and not being able to find anyone or any way to contact anyone on site.

8 DAY 5, IRONBRIDGE TO CULCHETH

It was a cold night, and a bad nights sleep. The cold woke me a few times, my aching back a few times more. I was decidedly grumpy as I made myself down a few cereal bars and the remains of the banana loaf from the previous night, it felt like it was going to be a long day. Creaking and groaning I made my way out of the tent and stretched, painfully, trying to wake my back up. I wasn't sure why it was hurting, if it was the cycling, the camping, the cold…or all three. Apart from that I felt in reasonable shape as I packed up my tent and supplies, being thankful for another dry morning at least.

Once on the bike and out of the campsite (still meeting nobody, I'd given in and paid online by this point) I carried on up the winding little lane I'd been on yesterday. I'd love to have gone back down into the town for breakfast, but it was a diversion and a hill I really couldn't face. Heading up the lane would soon bring me onto the A4169 for a mile or two, before I'd veer off onto the A5223 and head north, to the west of Telford and continue on. Past that it looked a fairly simple choice of roads as I'd work up to Warrington, Wigan, and then between Liverpool and Manchester as best I could to avoid the worst of the traffic. Planned!

Following my route, which was a little trickier than I'd imagined, wound me through a small housing estate before heading back out into the country lanes. I could see the road I planned to join but cursed to myself as it became clear the lane I was on, carried on right over my chosen road with no way to join. I stopped on the bridge to see if there was any way to sneak my way down the side of the bank, but there wasn't, the drop was much too large and severe. Frustrated I consulted my map again and found that I'd have to stick with my little lanes through several small villages, Little Wenlock and Huntington, before finally getting onto a 'proper road' west of Telford. Carrying on, and with my legs and back mercifully starting to co-operate, I tried to brush off the rather frustrating start to the day.

As I passed through Lawley, around an hour into the day, I stopped at a small shop in an attempt to refill my panniers a little. Complete waste of time, hands down the worst shop visited the whole trip, which could only describe as looking like it had just been cleared out after some apocalyptic end of the world type scenario had struck. I snatched up what little suitable food there was and headed on my way, thankful that Bants had at least survived on his own outside. Continuing my rather poor start to the day, I then got myself lost in a very confusing little housing estate once more, before finally getting onto a real road that was heading in the direction I actually wanted to be heading in! Yes! It's only been an hour I told myself, forget about that and move on.

Move on I did, escaping Telford (which was rather larger than expected) before spotting my favourite piece of roadside scenery for the trip, a burger bar! After the lack of hot food the previous night and during the morning, I had no second thoughts about stopping for a massive burger and onions whilst also picking up a few niceties for the pannier. My roadside cook / newest friend gets top marks for being a proper 'friend of the cyclists' as he told me all about the other 'end to enders' he'd met during the summer (that's good I thought, must be on a vaguely sensible route) while also not charging me a great deal for what was some very tasty food that improved my mood no end! Thankyou sir!

Back underway again and enjoying flat roads, I was a much happier cyclist as I continued north, up the A442 and then the A53 and A529 past Market Drayton. Only the lure of lunch stopped me at Audelm, where I also found a decent sized Co-op so the panniers got a proper re-filling! As I rode on into the afternoon I passed through a few slightly larger towns, Nantwich, Northwich, by this time the places were beginning to merge into one for me. The only use these unknown places were to me was as a target. I'd typically pick a town 20 miles or so ahead of me and keep chipping away until I reached it. There'd be no fanfare, celebration or reward when I arrived, in fact normally I'd blow straight through the place without even stopping, barely looking to the sides of the road in front of me, most likely never to return again. Once out of the town it would disappear in the road signs behind me, the distances back to it growing further and further until eventually it was deemed too far away, too insignificant for a place on the road signs. Not that I cared, I was already counting down the miles to the next town, the next target.

As I moved further into the afternoon, and the skies continued to darken, I entered Warrington on the A49. Warrington seemed to be quite a busy place and I was happy to find a few cycle paths along wide pavements, as the roads got progressively busier and multi-laned during the centre of the city. Once through the worst of it I pulled over into a garage for a sandwich and to figure out where I'd be staying that night. After the excitement / worry of not being able to find anywhere to stay for so long the previous day, I'd decided from then on that I'd get to 4 or 5pm each day and then check my phone for any local campsites, or B&B's if the weather was bad. As I munched on my sandwich outside the garage and beside a dual carriageway (glamorous business this long distance touring) I reasoned that although it was a little early to be looking for somewhere, it was currently dry and the forecast gave rain coming in by the evening. I like to think I'm reasonably good at reading what the weather is going to do in the short term after working outdoors for so many years, and I agreed with the forecast!

With that in mind I began looking for campsites and settled on one 6 miles to the north, Lanyards Farm Campsite. After a quick phone call to check that they were open year round, I finished my sandwich and set off towards that nights stop.

Now, by this point you'd have heard me moan about the cycling function on the Google Navigation App several times, and now be prepared for me to moan about it some more. In fairness this time it wasn't purely the apps fault, as far as it was concerned it was taking me down a road, well a lane, which was good enough for cars. But it wasn't. I was only a few miles from the campsite when the lane I turned onto, which looked fine from the end, turned into a muddy, waterlogged, rut filled, potholed, cobblestoned nightmare. I persevered for a little while before getting off and pushing, weaving my way through the worst of the water in an attempt not to have to put up with soaking wet trainers the next day....they were bad enough as it was!

With the dodgy lane behind me I enjoyed my last mile on a smooth road, before turning off into the campsite. Hurray it was still dry! A huge gate was blocking the entrance to the campsite, but soon enough I was spotted and the helpful chap I'd spoken to on the phone earlier appeared and showed me around. Once he found out about the trip (again, the bike is a bit of a giveaway) and that I was raising money for charity, he insisted that I stay for free. What a nice chap. He then went even further and gave me a quid for the showers as I didn't have any change on me, top man.

As light rain began to fall, my newest friend from my favourite campsite headed off and I quickly threw the tent up. In an effort to keep the bike as dry as possible (and feeling I'd probably pushed my luck enough at this particular site!) I buried it into the thick leafy hedge behind my tent and locked it to the fence, reasoning that it could stand a little rain, it had got completely drenched on day one after all! With the rain worsening I ran for the showers, they were perhaps a little more 'rustic' than some of the super posh campsites, but they did the trick and a shower always left me feeling a million times better afterwards.

One benefit to the rain, I thought, zipping myself back up in the tent, was that the temperature was a lot more manageable. I hoped for a much better nights sleep as a result, although I did still have a few hours to kill before it was time for sleep, even though I'd by now completely adopted 'farmers hours' and just slept when it was dark. It was 5:30pm so with the remaining few hours of daylight I did what was fast becoming the routine, planned out the next days route as much as possible, pigged out on food from the panniers, and spoke to the handful of people who knew I was currently in a tent near Wigan. Wigan I thought, nearly Liverpool and Manchester. Living in Devon my whole life that's always seemed like a long way. I quickly did a rough Google search of how far it was to Gretna Green, the furthest southern place in Scotland that immediately came to mind. A smile spread across my face, I could be in Scotland in two days. How crazy would that be, to have ridden to Scotland! I plugged my phone into its charger, snuggled down in my sleeping bag, prayed my back wouldn't kill me in the morning, and drifted off to sleep listening to the rain gently drop onto the tent. Scotland.

Distance Travelled – 73 Miles
Hedgerows Watered – 2 (9 Total)
Times shouted at Google Maps – 1 (4 Total)

Campsite 7/10 – Okay so it's not the poshest campsite, the toilets and showers are dated and coin operated, but it's clean and tidy, quiet, and run by a very nice chap, it deserves at least a 7 from my experience.

9 DAY 6, CULCHETH TO WINDERMERE

I woke a few times during the night, that's not unusual, I do at home too, but when it was finally late enough to get moving, I was annoyed to find that my back had once again set overnight. It was a sharp pain now, enough that my first attempt to sit up had resulted in me making a pathetic noise and laying right back down again. Taking a few breathes, I instead rolled myself onto my side and then into a sitting position, thanking god that my tent had enough headroom to allow that. Once sat up I took a few minutes to eat some breakfast, well, obligatory cereal bars, cakes, jam tarts, whatever my hands could reach without moving too much really. With that taken care of I struggled into my Lycra, never an easy job in a tent but made so much worse when you've ended up on your back like some sort of beached turtle. It'll get better in a little while I told myself, you just need to get moving.

So, get moving I did, retrieving Bants from the hedge, loading him up and setting off. I knew I had to get through Wigan just a few miles in, so was glad to be underway reasonably early, getting through that challenge before rush hour seemed like a good idea! As was becoming a pattern, I gradually loosened up once I was on the bike and by the time I hit Wigan I was feeling acceptable, not amazing but acceptable. More good news came as the busy traffic filled maze that I was expecting to find in Wigan never materialised, I passed straight through with no problems at all. The only slight blot on my morning was the torrential rain which seemed to have come out of nowhere. Despite having my waterproofs on, I still decided to stop for a minute at a garage for a celebratory pasty and bar of chocolate. Well, part celebration at getting through Wigan so easily, part wanting to get out of the freezing rain. I also took the opportunity to really study the next portion of my route, as in the bad weather I'd had to hide my phone in its waterproof bag in my top tube bag, meaning it was out of sight. Luckily with Wigan behind me my route for the day was pretty simple, mostly following the A6 which would run closely to the M6, taking me north through Preston and up to the Lake District. If this road was too busy I knew there were a few options of roads running parallel to it in reserve too, so I felt pretty comfortable with the days route.

With route committed to memory, food eaten, and messages checked, I decided I couldn't justify staying under the garages cover any longer, so I grudgingly made my way through the forecourt and back out into the freezing rain. Why does it always seem so much worse after you've stopped too? Still, on the positive side brighter skies were ahead, the road seemed good and I was making progress. Half an hour later the rain had stopped which improved my mood further still, as I powered on with my back also feeling better with every passing mile, another massive relief. After the pain I'd felt first thing in the morning, I'd half been expecting the day to be a write off, but as it turned out it was a solid two hour stint between leaving the garage and my next stop, a last minute decision to grab some early lunch at a Spar in Bamber Bridge. I felt good to carry on but hadn't seen too many shops all day so decided to have something while it was on offer. The 'something' on offer was a rather dodgy combination sandwich, the worst of the three being a rather suspect looking prawn one. I ate it anyway whilst thinking it was probably a bad idea, then looked at the packet and realised it was out of date, lovely!

Back on the bike and not feeling the sandwich had done the trick, I stopped at a burger van set up in a layby half an hour later. Well, I wasn't really having too many proper dinners, so I liked to get something reasonably close to real food at some point during the day. Having completely failed to get a conversation going with one of the grumpiest people I met during the whole trip (and a complete opposite to all the other friendly burger van owners encountered) I gave up and played with my phone while he cooked. It must be said he did redeem himself somewhat by making a properly good burger and cup of tea! Fuelled up once more I set off again, this time feeling uncomfortably full….perfect! That was a feeling that would soon pass though, far better to eat too much than too little.

The roads continued to be good and largely flat, and although I didn't seem to be having any assistance from the wind it didn't seem to be hindering me either. In fact the only thing that was hindering me was the lack of anywhere to stop for a pee. When I'd needed to go during the previous week, it had often been a quick dash into the trees or behind a hedge out of view of the road, as it just wasn't practical to keep diverting into towns and trying to find toilets…it would have added hours and countless miles. It hadn't so far been a problem to find somewhere discreetly out of the way but that was not proving the case now! Mile after mile of road with only a two foot wide strip of grass and a solid hedge besides it. Well, at a certain point when you've got to go you've got to go, so I hope any passing motorists had a good laugh at the cyclist clearly pissing behind a tree at the side of the A6.

Not so discreet pee taken care of and I gave the rear tyre a quick squeeze before getting back on, as it had been feeling soft for a couple hundred yards before stopping. Hmm, a squeeze definitely confirmed it was running soft. I was getting very bored of punctures by this point, so as the tyre was still holding air I decided to pump it back up again, and see if it could at least make the end of the day when I'd change it at the campsite. Tyre inflated and I set off again, but 10 minutes or so later and I was forced to stop once more as it felt like I was riding on a squishy marshmallow. Bugger. I pulled Bants up onto a small pathway on the side of a bridge and flipped him over. Glancing over the side of the bridge for a second I saw that it was crossing a canal, with the boats passing below me. I watched them, thinking it looked quite a peaceful way to spend some time and that I must try it sometime. Then I remembered I was in the middle of a daft challenge already and continued on changing my puncture. Further back down the road and another cyclist was approaching, but a big thumbs down to him as he passed without offering any assistance or so much as a nod. Poor form. Any time I've ever had a problem or quickly stopped for something so small as adjusting a seat, I've never had another cyclist pass without at least a quick 'Ok?' There's generally a really good camaraderie among cyclists and I was pleased when the next one along stopped to make sure I had everything I needed. "Of course you do with all the gear you've got there" he laughed, "probably got enough to build a spare bike!" So thankyou to random cyclist man who stopped on the bridge just past Garstang, much appreciated.

Puncture repaired and I was soon flying along again, really flying in fact, I began to wonder if I'd been running on a low pressure all day. Either that or I'd picked up a bit of assistance from the wind. With good speed, good weather, and air in my tyres I was a happy traveller as I continued north, past endless fields, small farmhouses and industrial units, huge ice-cream shops with gigantic cones outside, and a list of flavours so long you'd need half an hour to make a choice, more fields…… Wait! I've nearly made it to

Scotland without an ice-cream! Deciding that had to be put right I double backed on myself and lent Bants up against the shop as I ordered a giant Eton Mess ice-cream in a waffle cone, perfection. I greedily dug in like a child and had a fit of the giggles that I'd ridden my pushbike nearly as far as Scotland. Serious chap me! As usual it didn't take long for Bants to attract some attention, as two middle aged chaps wandered over to ask if I was cycling the end to end. Turns out they had both completed it the previous month as part of an organised group. They'd had set accommodation at the end of each day and a support van to carry equipment. I nodded along as they told me of their trip, including some horrendous sounding weather which I hoped to continue mostly avoiding, despite doing the trip later in the year. I'd rather be lucky than talented any day! As we swapped stories I'm ashamed I did keep thinking, 'cheats, pairs of cheats, not carrying anything, organised routes, warm bed and meal prepared at the end of the day' which isn't entirely fair. To cycle that far is a massive achievement however you do it, but as a solo cyclist I do admit to turning up my nose up ever so slightly at the organised groups. I apologise but I just do, even if deep down I think they're the sensible ones!

My giant ice-cream was taking some time to eat, and I began to think that stopping may have been a mistake as the skies around me darkened. Giving myself brain freeze I hastily finished my ice-cream and set off while the going was still good, maybe there had been too many stops today? It had just gone 1pm so I decided that mileage wise it was going okay, but that I should make an effort to get a couple solid hours in. Luckily that's exactly what I managed, the threatening skies coming to nothing, the roads staying reasonably flat and me not getting distracted by food stops or punctures! Well, not for a couple hours anyway until I pulled over at an Esso Garage on the edge of Gait Barrows National Nature Reserve. It was a very quick stop though, just long enough to eat a chicken wrap and packet of crisps, while stowing a few more treats into my pannier for later use.

With it still being reasonably early at just gone 3pm, I decided to get a few more miles in before searching for a campsite for the night. Another quiet 6 miles on the trusty A6 followed after leaving the garage, until all hell broke loose. My beautiful road just sort of, stopped. All I was left with was little more than a lane that headed into the Lake District, in nowhere near the direction I wanted to go, or a slip road up a hill towards what sounded like a dual carriageway. Sitting at the bottom of the slip road I stared at my map, willing some magical third choice to appear, but it didn't happen. I dithered, then I dithered some more before finally heading up the slip road to take a look at how bad the road was. Reaching the top of the wide slip road gave me my answer. Bad. I checked my map again but there was still no magic road to get me out of this mess. No 'A26 – Deserted road for Ross blessed with beautiful weather, a constant tail wind and no cars.' Shame, could have used one of those. Finally deciding I had no option, I gritted my teeth, swore that if I killed myself doing this I'd be very annoyed with myself, and resigned myself to a couple dodgy miles until I could reach a safer road.

I will say this, the noise of rapidly approaching dual carriageway traffic does provide an excellent incentive to go quickly. I roared along like a rider in the Tour de France, whilst making use of every layby and strip of extra tarmac I could to get out of the way. A mile in and the A590 which I was now on, merged with another road and became the A591, which was also terrible and again the only real option. Mercifully there was only another mile or so on this road before I found an exit, which I decided to take no matter where I had to go as this road was going from bad to ridiculous. Pulling up just off the exit slip I breathed heavily and had a long drink, without doubt the previous few miles had been the hardest I'd tried all trip. Now though, I had a problem. Since that road was clearly out I needed a new plan. One that would get me to where I wanted to be as quickly as possible, but also allow me to arrive there alive and in one piece. More map staring followed. Two options. The first and original plan was to stick with the A6, which had now reappeared at the end of the slip road I was currently sat on, this would take me in a straight northerly direction as far as Carlisle. It stuck close to the M6 for most parts and I figured that should make it fairly quiet. But I'd just been massively freaked out by it suddenly turning into dual carriageways, and realised that if it did that after I passed Kendal in a few miles time I'd be stuck with it for miles, there were just no other options except to turn around. My other option was to use the A6 through Kendal where it was quiet, before ducking back out onto the previously dodgy A591. This then headed right into the Lake District and soon after I'd be off into smaller roads anyway, to take me north to Carlisle. I knew enough to know this route would at least involve no major dual carriageways, very little traffic at all in fact, but would likely be steeper, and longer, but certainly more beautiful. Longer and longer I sat, still unsure what to do. As in all truly desperate 'I don't know what to do' situations, I rang Dad to ask if he knew what the A6 was like in that part of the country. I don't remember the exact conversation, I think even Uncle Bob may have weighed in with an opinion, as he was with Dad at the time. Hanging up and I was still unsure what to do, only now with the added annoyance of light rain now starting to fall. A quick search for a campsite revealed that the Windermere Camping and Caravan Site was the closest and only real option, the fact that it was also situated on the A591 route option through the Lake District, also helped make my route decision for me! Sometimes just making the decision can make you feel better, after so long just sat being indecisive it felt great to be moving again, as I completed the last 6 miles of the day towards that nights campsite. Sure enough there was a little dual carriageway involved, but it was much quieter now this side of Kendal, and I could see there wouldn't be any more than a mile or two of it to contend with in the morning. As I turned off the dual carriageway and followed the campsite signs down a small lane, I was happy to be arriving. It wasn't particularly late at only just gone 5pm but it had felt like a long day, the dark skies and overhanging trees making it feel much later as I finally emerged at the site entrance. Bliss.

It really was bliss too, it seems I'd inadvertently stumbled across campsite perfection in the Lake District. Firstly, the receptionists were wonderful friendly people, who only went up in my estimation as firstly they only charged me £6, as they decided cyclists counted as backpackers (close enough) and then told me there was an onsite pub that would be opening soon and provided dinner and desserts! Sold! Number one campsite of the trip. Determined to get to dinner as quickly as possible, I chucked the tent up in the most protected corner available, then made my way to the showers. They were excellent of course, everything here was. Coming back from the showers I stumbled across the 'backpackers cabin', a small wooden cabin equipped with tables, chairs and a functional kitchen for use by the backpackers. As it was October and the site was largely empty (aside from a few caravans) I went and retrieved Bants from the fence I'd tied him to, and instead locked him up in the cabin for the night so he could stay dry. With him happy, I stopped off at the tent and grabbed my backup batteries to charge while I was in the pub. One glance at the menu and I found my go to comfort order, Lasagne, which would be followed by a large chocolate cake served with ice-cream. Have I mentioned this was the best campsite of the trip yet? It really was. Just being sat in the warm, with some good food and some electric to charge my batteries, while I got my phone out and chatted with my friends was the perfect end to the day. In fact I'd quite happily have stayed there all night, as once I went back outside it really had turned cold, and for the first time I was feeling it as I climbed into my tent, added a hoodie over my jumper and pulled my sleeping bags tightly around me. A couple minutes of shivering resumed until the temperature reached a decent enough level to allow me to fall asleep. Fall asleep on my side this time in a desperate attempt to not wake up paralysed and frozen the next morning!

Distance Travelled – 75 Miles
Hedgerows watered – 1 (10 Total)
Punctures – 1 (5 Total)
Ridiculously cold nights – 1 (2 Total)

Campsite – 10/10 – Perfection! What else can I say about this campsite? Stunning location, quiet, beautifully kept with great facilities, pub on site and one of the cheapest stays of the trip. Very tempted to borrow my parents camper van at some point in the future and base it here while I spend a few days exploring the Lake District.

Above – Training in the stunning Exmoor Beauty sportive in early 2017. Below – Shortly before leaving John O'Groats on the first attempt.

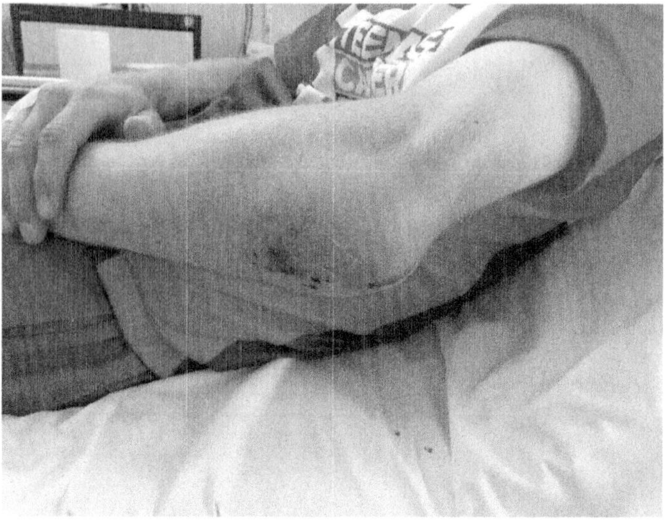

Above – At Wick, a couple of hours after the crash.
Below – In Inverness hospital the day after my operation.

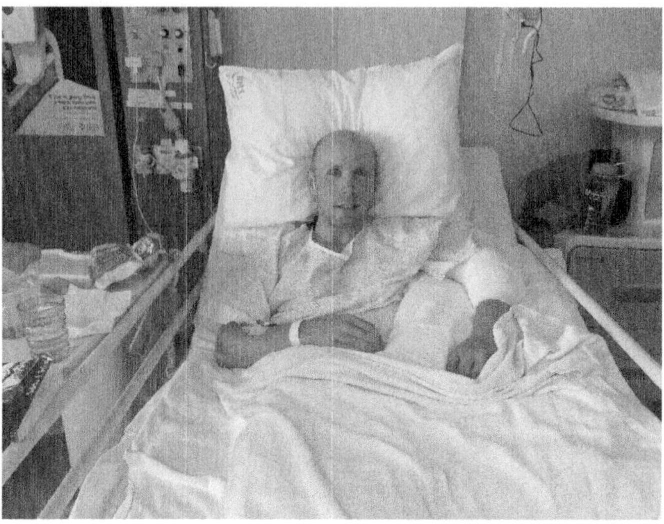

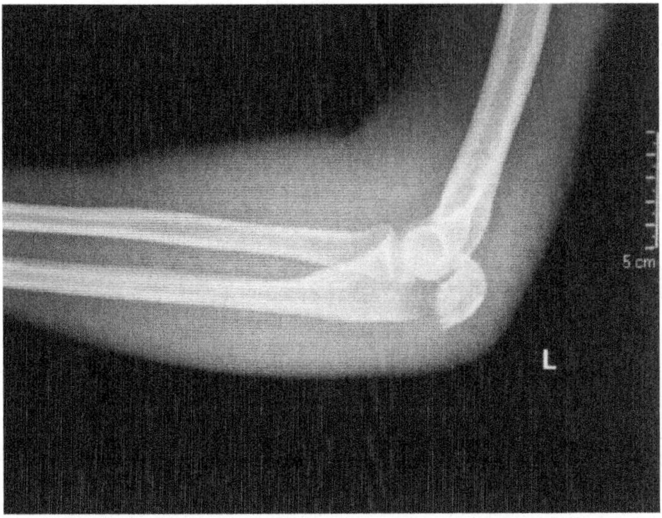

Before and after X-rays of my elbow. The surgeons at Raigmore hospital in Inverness did a great job, look at those pins!

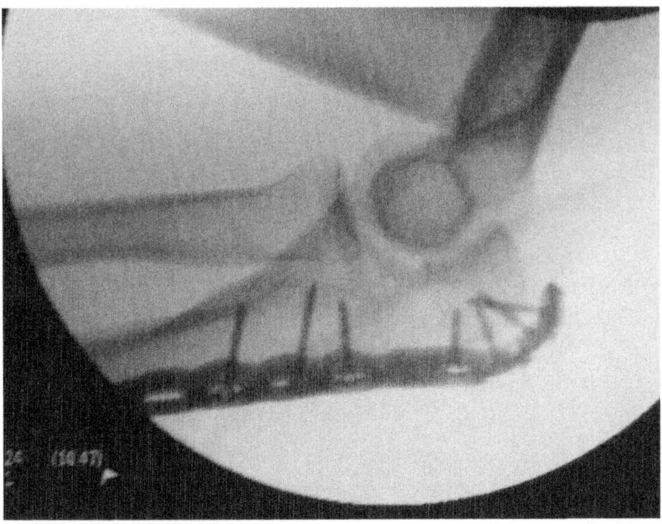

Above – Waiting at Newton Abbot train station.
Below – Land's End on the morning of day 1. Getting ready to go!

At the very start of my adventure…attempt number two. No trailer, no huge announcement, just me and Bants and a select few people 'in the know'. What an amazing few weeks were ahead of us.

Above – St.Michael's Mount in Cornwall on day 1.
Below – On the way into Portreath before the heavy rain arrived.

Above – Not a bad view with a bacon sandwich.
Below – Bants and my marvelous tent in Taunton at the end of day 2.

Above – Welcome to Shropshire. Below – One of the many roadside burger 'vans' which kept me going throughout the trip.

Above – Feeling tired in the beautiful Lake District.
Below – Food stop at the cutest little Post Office / stores in Patterdale.

Above – Scotland! Yes! The relief was incredible. Below – The isolated 'ghost road' on the first day in Scotland. It was a very quiet day.

Above – How could I not stop for a photo? Below – The final morning. Stunning roads, weather, and the finish in sight. Perfection.

Above – I made it! Me and Bants arrived in John O'Groats against the odds on day 12. Below – A little snap of Orkney, calmer than it was for the crossing!

10 DAY 7, WINDERMERE TO GRETNA GREEN

It was not a good nights sleep. It had been cold. Very cold. Ridiculously cold. The problem with being too cold is that it's just impossible to sleep, your body keeps waking you up to tell you it's cold. One positive to come from being awake every half an hour all night, was that I'd moved all night, and when it was finally time to give in on getting any more sleep and I attempted to get up, I found that my back was feeling much better than it had the previous few mornings. I sat up without having to resort to holding my breath or letting out a single yelp, yes this was much better! There was no way I could face getting even partially undressed in the cold tent to get into my lycra though, so I gathered everything up and headed off to the toilets. Swinging the doors open and the heat from inside found me instantly, giving me one of the best and most welcome hugs I've had in my life. I seriously regretted not just hiding out in there all night.

After thawing for 10 minutes in the warm toilets I was a much happier camper when I re-emerged, making a quick dash across the frost covered lawn to retrieve Bants from the backpackers cabin. Another place warmer than my tent, I thought to myself as I freed Bants and squeezed him through the door. Back at the tent I began packing up while downing a few cereal bars, despite not feeling all that hungry. Having a proper meal for once the night before was obviously helping, but I knew I still had to have something. I told myself I'd stop at the first place available to get something slightly more interesting to eat.

Although the weather had been dry overnight, everything was covered in frost and packing up was frustrating and time consuming, especially as my fingers were starting to go numb. This had definitely been the coldest night so far, I prayed it wouldn't get any worse in Scotland. If it did I'd need to start finding more B&B's, which could be quite a challenge in the rural areas I'd be cycling in later on in the trip.

With everything packed up, I jumped on and set off down the lane from the campsite at a reasonably quick pace. Normally I make an effort to really try and ease into the first few miles of the day, but I was just eager to work some warmth into myself on such a cold day. Halfway down the lane I turned off onto another road I'd noticed on my map the previous night, which saved a little bit of distance and joined me back onto the A591 slightly later on than I would have, where I was pleased to find that it was no longer a dual carriageway! Fantastic, a plan had worked! This was celebration time and a trip to the next garage for a large BLT sandwich and scotch egg was in order. I sat outside as I ate, leaning against the shopfront and tried to wrap my head around the fact that I should be in Scotland by the end of the day. Scotland. Amazing. I wiped the smile off my face, well aware that nothing was done until it was done, and carried on.

Not having to creak and groan my back into action for the first few miles was a real morale booster, as was spotting a little shortcut on my map a few miles later. I was currently travelling in an annoying west direction and would be for a few miles further, until reaching Lake Windermere when I would again be able to head north. But the little lane I'd spotted on the map would cut the Windermere corner off, letting me travel northwest now and join the A592 higher up. Yes, good news. Crossing the wide A591 I headed off up my little lane. Up being the word as there was no denying I was in the Lake District now, there would be climbing. After being so cold just a few miles earlier, I found myself stopping to remove a layer after a short hill. The problem with lots of ascents and descents on a bike, is that you just can't keep yourself at a happy temperature. You struggle uphill, working up a sweat as you work hard, and then you all but roll down the other side, suddenly not working and now rushing through the cold air at 20mph, as you struggle to keep enough feeling in your hands to work the brakes. You can't win.

Shortcut complete and I joined the A592, merrily cycling along admiring the stunning scenery. This was a real few moments of utter bliss and enjoyment at being on this bike, at this moment in time, in this place doing this challenge. Then the hill started....and didn't let up. Looking back at the ride data, it shows the Kirkstone Pass area I was struggling up to be barely over 3 miles....it felt more like 30. Cycling it was right out for the most part, it was just far too steep. Relentlessly steep, with rivers of water, mud and gravel washing across the road from the surrounding hills. I pushed, pushed and pushed some more. I swore, I pushed, I pushed and I swore. Every time it seemed we might be nearing the top, the road curved around and presented me with yet more climbing. This was a struggle, Bants was so heavy that pushing him for so long was a major effort uphill. Such an effort that I deemed a Mars bar necessary and went diving into the pannier after one. Finally, mercifully, the road began to level out as I neared the summit, but the headwinds were so strong that I was still swapping between pushing and cycling at walking speed whilst struggling. My route choice got questioned more than once as I continued on, but even I had to see the funny side when I spotted a sign just before the top, 'Ambleside' it read, 'Via The Struggle.' I believe this was referring to the road next to mine but it looked similar.

From the top of the Kirkstone Pass you can see an amazing road laid out before you, snaking its way down the valley. With a final turn of the pedals I gave Bants a bit of momentum to get him moving, then settled in for a few highly enjoyable and 'free' miles. It had been two and a half hours since I'd left the campsite and I'd only covered 11 miles. That's how slow progress had been so the dash down the valley, whilst very cold, was much appreciated, and great fun as I took all the racing lines and lent Bants over as much as I dared in the corners. Eventually the 'down' ran out but at least I had a few more relatively gentle miles, before stopping at a small Post Office / Shop / Bakery / anything else the beautiful small village of Patterdale needed it to be. Despite being October a number of backpackers were milling around in the village, with a few more in the shop picking up a bacon baguette as I was. With so many backpackers and outdoor enthusiasts visiting the area, I found it to be very welcoming and well set up, even finding a toilet block hidden away behind the houses. Sitting down on a bench outside I admired my idyllic setting once more before checking my map. After leaving I would be skirting around the shores of Ullswater, where my attention was drawn to a number of kayakers having fun in the calm water. My mind was drawn back to my recent near drowning experience in my own Kayak, and I vowed to become a much better swimmer and to invest in a good lifejacket before I ever went near the thing again! With Ullswater behind me I turned off onto the A5091, which was steep but so stunning that I had to stop for a few more photos. This area of the country was definitely seeing more camera action than anywhere else I'd been so far! Passing through Matterdale and Troutbeck I then found myself briefly on a wonderful deserted road which ran beside the A66, before turning onto one of my absolute favourite stretches of the trip.

The strange thing about doing a long distance trip,

in my limited experience at least, is how just a few factors can either work with you, or against you, to make any given day or hour an absolute nightmare that leaves you questioning why you're doing it in the first place, or leave you thinking that you've made the best decision of your life. What really messes with your head is that you can very easily swing from one to the other within a few hours. For instance, whereas just a few hours earlier I'd been struggling up an impossible hill getting nowhere, and the day before I'd been dodging cars on a dodgy road, I now found myself in cycling nirvana. The road I joined from the A66 was already quiet, very quiet, as it thread its way past fields and farms, but as I carried on it just got better and better. I passed through wonderful little villages, Mungrisdale, Bowscale and countless others, as the road continued to shrink until the point where I began to question if it even was a road any more. It was still perfectly smooth, it just wasn't any wider than a car, and there were a complete lack of cars. Pedalling on, it seemed the only reason anyone drove along it, was to park up and take their dogs for a walk in the perfect surroundings. Aside from them it was just me and a few other cyclists, the luckiest cyclists in the world it must be said if they could include this stretch as part of their routine ride. I stopped and had some lunch under the beautiful blue skies and tried to really remember this place, these were parts of the trip I really didn't want to forget.

Lunch over and Hesket Newmarket struck me as the next stunning little place I passed through, with its small village green and polite nods and good mornings from friendly dog walkers in abundance. The road continued to rise and fall but I didn't mind. I even didn't mind when I had to do a bit of an awkward zig zag after Caldwell, as there just weren't any roads to go in the direction I wanted to be heading. Okay, maybe I minded crawling along a little bit as I changed to the B5299, but seven hours into the day (and an embarrassing 40 miles) I reached the top of another long climb and spotted what had to be Carlisle off in the distance. Carlisle, that's nearly Scotland I thought to myself excitedly. Many memories of my home town football club, Torquay United, making the long trip to Carlisle came flooding back, often the longest trip in league football…until we lost the plot and went crashing out of the league that is, but that's another story for another book. Anyway, Carlisle nearly being Scotland, that's what matters now I thought as I set off, greedily taking advantage of the downhill section, swooping towards my target through the village of Welton which had a beautiful curve to the road. A beautiful curve with a lot of loose gravel I realised…I spotted a larger piece just ahead of my front tyre but there was no time to go around it, not without chucking myself on the floor anyway, so I gritted my teeth (vitally important) and bounced over it. Slightly uncomfortable perhaps but at least everything was okay, except that squishy feeling front end. Oh no.

I pulled up at the side of the road with my rim already on the floor, the now airless inner tube in my front tyre doing me no good whatsoever. A front puncture. I'd never seen a front puncture on a bike before, you just always get them at the rear where all weight is, never the front. The spare inner tubes I'd picked up at my auntie and uncles were still in my pannier, and at least it was dry, my only concern other than the waste of time was the front pannier mounts. I'd fitted them in a bit of a rush just before leaving, and hadn't considered whether or not I'd be able to get the skewer out of the front wheel with them fitted. I also knew that I didn't have the right size spanner, or even a pair of pliers to remove them with. Flipping the bike over in the soft grass, I first disconnected the bags themselves from the lower mount by the wheel skewer. This was difficult enough as I'd cable tied them on and in the absence of any proper cutters, had to wear the cable tie through by rubbing it against the edge of the metal mount. With that time consuming job done the bags themselves could at least be pulled out of the way. It was fiddly but I was immensely relieved to find out that there was just about enough room to get the spindle out, with the pannier mount itself still attached. If not I'd have had to go begging at some houses until I found somebody with a toolkit! Wheel out and I swapped the punctured tube for a new one before putting everything back together. I'd definitely gotten lazy again when it came to doing tyre pressures every morning, especially on the front, so I again vowed to do this every morning whether the tyre felt deflated at all or not. I certainly felt deflated as I put Bants back the right way up and got moving again. What a waste of half an hour, and another inner tube I thought, I'd need to stop and get some more before getting into rural Scotland…all because I couldn't be bothered to spend a few minutes in the cold this morning pumping up tyres….silly boy.

After a bit of a pep talk (come on man you're nearly in Scotland) I got a bit of a spurt on and made my way into Carlisle. I wasn't sure what to expect but from what I saw it seemed like quite a nice place, as I hurriedly sped my way past a Cathedral and a Castle, before crossing over the River Eden. Just as I was making my way out of the far side of Carlisle, I began thinking that it would have been a good idea to find somewhere to eat back in town, I hadn't had a great deal today. Then I spotted a Greggs perched bizarrely in the middle of an industrial estate off to my right. Perfect! Having never been to a Greggs before it felt like somewhere I should go too. (I'm a proper southerner don't forget, we didn't get them for ages.)

Many calories later and I was moving again, picking up the B7076. It sounds sad (well it just is actually) but I was very excited to get onto this road as I was planning on following it for over 60 miles up towards Glasgow. I'd chosen this road as it stuck very close to the M74, so I reasoned it should be very quiet with all the regular traffic opting for the faster motorway. That certainly seemed to be the case, as Carlisle disappeared behind me as I cycled up this magical road all by myself. Just the other side of a small fence and a piece of grass I could see the busy motorway, but on my side nothing at all, just smooth empty tarmac. Another few miles of this please! Being properly ready to get into Scotland now I stared longingly at every sign that came into view, willing it to be a 'Welcome to Scotland' message. Sign after sign passed but still nothing. This was getting frustrating. I knew Gretna Green was just over the border, so I'd started counting down the miles to there instead and it was getting so close. Just a couple more miles to go and with the weather on the turn, I decided to find a campsite for the night now in case I had to hide my phone away from the rain. Literally any campsite as long as it's over that border I thought to myself, as I began searching Google. After ruling a few out for being too far away or too off course, I settled on one that was perhaps a little closer than I'd have liked, although on the plus side it looked to be no more than a couple hundred metres off route and only a few miles past Gretna Green. That'll do, so long as it's in Scotland, early-ish finish deserved today of all days.

Back underway again and within a few minutes I'd found my sign. I'd been looking forward to seeing it for nearly 600 miles and couldn't help but think it would vanish when I got close like some sort of mirage, or I'd wake up from a dream and find myself back in my tent in Cornwall. But no, I rolled up to the sign and actually touched it, it was there. I was in Scotland. I'd cycled to Scotland and only a handful of people knew! Brilliant! The particular 'Welcome to Scotland' sign I'd found on my road was fairly modest, and annoyingly had steps in front of it which I had to lift Bants up to lean him against the sign itself. But it was here, and I snapped so many cheesy pics of both me and the bike, and one very over excited video. I'm sure any passers-by found it slightly amusing but I just didn't care, I was here, next stop John O'Groats!

Photo session over and I decided to make my way to the campsite while it was still dry. Passing through

Gretna Green was a pleasant experience, before I encountered an incredibly straight couple miles of gentle climb on the other side, which I was helped up immensely by being able to sit in the slipstream of a very nice mountain biker. Thankyou sir! At the top of the gentle climb I stopped at a tiny shop in Kirkpatrick-Flemming to try and pick up something for dinner. It was very slim pickings in the shop, and although I'd just crossed the border everything suddenly felt very Scottish, even the broad accent of the cashier reminded me how far I'd come, causing me to break out in a huge smile. The woman must have been wondering why some knackered looking cyclist was stood grinning like an idiot, so I explained where I'd come from and how happy I was to have made it far enough to encounter a Scottish accent. She wished me luck and now only a two minute ride stood between me and the bizarrely named King Robert the Bruce caravan park and camp site.

Cycling into the site involved passing a very grand old house and several life-size statues of lions and men in armour, riding horses and swinging swords. How bizarre. I spied the reception building and made my way over to it, only to find it was locked. A note on the door displayed a mobile number to ring, but as I was doing so I was spotted by someone who came over to book me in for the night. He explained that the site was set in the grounds of Cove Estate and featured Bruce's' cave, an ancient monument from the 14th century where King Bruce hid for three months during the Scottish wars of Independence, apparently. My tour guide then seamlessly slid from stories of 14th century kings, to showing me where the toilets and amenities were located. It all seemed very strange but you have to hand it to them for having something very unique about their campsite…it's not one that I'll easily forget! Despite all the history my eyes were only drawn to one thing on my quick tour, a bath. A huge inviting looking bath that had my eye from the second I saw it. A bath was just what my aching body needed. Returning to Bants I wanted to get my tent up quickly while it was still dry, again amazed at how the rain was generally managing to hold off until I arrived at a campsite each night. Long may this continue!

Forgive me but I'm going to talk about bowel movements for a second now, so feel free to skim a paragraph if you so wish. I'm not someone who has to rush to the toilet several times a day, or ever with any urgency, but I did think I could do with going once I'd put my tent up. Then that I had to go now. Right now. Leaving the tent where I'd thrown it, surrounded by items I'd been pulling out of the panniers, I headed straight for the toilets with great pace. Immense pace in fact. If you've ever seen the hilarious toilet scene from the film 'Bridesmaids' then picture that. Flinging the door to the toilet open I dashed inside, already fumbling with waterproofs, jogging bottoms, lycra…..why was I wearing so many layers! It was close. I very nearly made my entrance into Scotland by crapping myself. This was far from good I thought as I sat on the toilet for far too long, literally unable to move too far, I couldn't be ill. Thinking about what I'd eaten during the day, nothing dodgy came to mind, and I'd been cycling for a week by this point so surely it couldn't be any effects of that.

When I did eventually dare to move I remembered all the items I'd left strewn across the grass outside in my rush, thankfully they were all still there. Gathering up my phone, charger and backup batteries first, I took these into the small laundrette / kitchen room and put them on charge. Having everything fully charged provided a strange amount of comfort I was coming to realise. I was completely reliant on my phone for so much, and knowing that I had the capability to keep it charged and on for up to a week with full batteries was always a plus. The previous night in the pub at Windermere had allowed me to nearly charge one battery, so I put this one on first to top up while having my bath, and would then put my second nearly flat battery on to charge overnight.

Electrics taken care of and I piled everything else I'd need for the night into the tent, before finally returning to that wonderful bath. Please be hot water, please be hot water I prayed to myself. There was. Endless amounts of it as I ran a huge bath and relaxed into it letting out a sigh. I could have stayed there all night, easily, as it was I was in there until the water started to go cold and I decided I'd better move. I cannot describe how wonderful it felt. Back outside and the overcast night meant that there would be no repeat of the freezing temperatures from the night before either, so there was a lot to be happy about as I settled down for sleep. Slightly concerned that I'd had to visit the toilet again but quite happy apart from that!

Distance Travelled – 63 Miles
Hedgerows watered – 1 (11 Total)
Punctures – 1 (6 Total)
Borders crossed – 1!

Campsite – 7/10 – Unique. If I had to summarise this campsite in one word it would certainly be unique. Aside from the interesting backstory and surroundings, the site itself is tidy enough. The toilet block is well kept and the facilities are good. The shop was shut when I arrived (which was perfectly understandable given the time of day / year) but looked to be well stocked.

11 DAY 8, GRETNA GREEN TO STRATHCLYDE

I'm in Scotland! My first thought upon waking up on Saturday morning, shortly followed by, I need the toilet! After several trips to the toilet during packing up and getting ready, I deemed myself ready to go, ready to leave this bizarre campsite behind me and hopefully not have to crap in the woods somewhere in the next few hours!

As I cycled out of the campsite and headed towards the train crossing I'd passed the previous evening, the lights flashed and the barrier came down in front of me. Perfect timing. I sat and waited for the train to appear which seemed to take an age. So long in fact that I took my phone off the handlebars and filmed one of my embarrassing videos. Looking at it now I seem mostly concerned with my toilet visits, and the fact that I'd left my Asos Chamois Cream (that's ass cream if you've forgotten) at Windermere the previous morning, a fact I'd only just discovered after completely emptying every bag I had with me desperately looking for it. But no, it wasn't there, it was beside the sink at Windermere campsite, where I'd put it down while I brushed my teeth. This concerned me. From a comfort point of view I'd felt reasonably okay so far which was a constant relief to me. I'd really expected to struggle to be in the saddle for 10 hours a day for 2 weeks, after being off the bike for 3 months beforehand, but after the first day or two everything seemed fine, I just hoped it would continue to be so without my magic cycling cream as I highly doubted I'd find a cycling shop any time soon. As I pondered this the train finally chugged past, so slowly that I probably could have jumped on if I'd so wished, before the gates raised and I could get my day underway.

Turning back onto the quiet B7076 from yesterday and it greeted me with every cyclists favourite thing, a tail wind! Shifting effortlessly up the gears I was flying along, soon putting 6 miles in the bag as I laughed my way through the hilariously named 'Ecclefechan'. Not even the large hill just past Ecclefechan could dampen my spirits, as I said the word out loud a few times to amuse myself. In truth I needed to amuse myself, as I really was on my own today. With Ecclefechan (snigger) behind me I seemed to enter into my own little world, the road was deserted to the point of only seeing a handful of cars every hour, there were no towns or villages and hence no pedestrians. The road sometimes came into view of the motorway, always sticking near it, but often it was shielded from view by large trees or hills when we did briefly separate. Eerie was certainly the word with the low mist adding to the remoteness. It must be said progress was amazing though which is always cause to be in a good mood, I just pressed on and hoped the tail wind would stick with me. After yesterday's slow progress through the hills of the Lake District, it would be nice to bag some real mileage today.

With the dodgy stomach in mind I hadn't had much for breakfast, but just over an hour and a half after leaving the campsite I was feeling okay, so stopped at Lockerbie Lorry Park for a quick bite to eat. I'd passed Lockerbie quite some distance earlier, but I guess with the sheer lack of towns in the area they'd just plumped for the nearest. A pasty, a bar of chocolate and an apple went down easily before moving off again, determined to make the most of my wind assisted morning. 18 miles down so far, many more to go.

That food stop seemed like a better and better idea the further I went, as there really wasn't anything else for hours. It was just me, my thoughts and my bike. On and on we went. Four hours and 35 miles into the day I stopped for a quick pee (they were easy in this deserted place) and then carried on. The road changed to the A702 but it still stayed quiet, always sticking close to the M74, occasionally crossing over or under it, but never straying too far from it. The river Clyde was also in view for some time until I finally rolled into another small town, Abingdon. I spotted a small shop / post office and went in to draw out some money (I was running low and finding that not everywhere accepted cards) and pick up some lunch. The usual whatever was available mix of sandwiches, sausage rolls, and lucky me my favourite chocolate bar of the moment, Hersheys Cookies and Cream. Top shop. I sat on a bench outside munching my way through my food, watching the world go by in another little place I'd surely never visit again. My phone said I'd now covered just over 45 miles, not bad going by 1pm. I hoped the afternoon would be as kind to me.

A slight bit of head scratching followed at the next couple roundabouts, as I had to get myself to the other side of the motorway and onto the B7078 to continue shadowing the M74 towards Glasgow. Once I'd managed that though it was plain sailing for another wonderful 20 miles, until I pulled over into a petrol station in Kirkmuirhill. The little Spar shop had a wonderful bakery so I had a good eat and then bought a huge amount of food, so much that it really was a struggle to get it into the pannier. After such a remote day though it really make sense to stay stocked up, especially as there was every chance I may have to do some wild camping towards the north of Scotland.

I'd noticed earlier on in the day that my route towards Glasgow had synced up with the National Cycle Route 74, and as I knew that headed straight into Glasgow I'd started relying on the signs as much as the navigation on my phone. It had been very sensibly signed all day, so when I spotted a sign telling me to turn off I went with it without too much hesitation, figuring that it was just going to be a small detour around a busy piece of road, or perhaps linking me to a bespoke cycle path as it had a couple times already. Wrong. I'd turned off my beautiful road, instead replacing it with a very hilly 6 miles of muddy lanes which wasted a great deal of time and effort, before emerging back on the B7078 in Larkhall. Silly move. Somewhere during my unintended detour I realised I'd also passed the 1000km mark for the trip so far. I took a screenshot and pressed on, knowing that the campsite I'd decided on back at the petrol station wasn't too far away now.

Through Alanton and then into the outskirts of Hamilton, it felt strange to actually be around people and busy roads again! Flicking to Google Maps I entered the details for Strathclyde Camping and Caravan site and then proceeded, as usual, to disagree with the route I was being presented with. I bounced through an industrial estate, along a narrow path beside a field, before emerging through a small wood onto a stunning cycle / footpath alongside Strathclyde Loch. It seems everyone from miles around descended on this one area and I had to travel slowly, picking my way through other cyclists, walkers, dogs, children, footballs, skateboarders, radio controlled cars. Literally any activity you could think of was being tried out here I thought, as I dodged a low flying kite.

Passing the end of the Loch, a small footpath led me out onto a road right opposite the campsite. Brilliant. First impressions of the campsite were slightly snobby but very well kept. The receptionist was lovely though, and soon checked me in and pointed me towards the area reserved for tents where I would again be the only one. That said she did tell me that someone stayed until November in a tent last year, so there are some people madder than me!

Despite the perfect lawns and very smart buildings, the campsite couldn't escape the fact that it was rather too close to the M74, so I placed my tent to the side of a closed shower block, using it as a bit of a sound barrier. Yes that works quite well I thought, stepping around the corner away from my shielded tent. With Bants locked up to the side of the building and my tent stocked up for the night, I went for a shower (no bath tonight) and reflected on what had been a good day. There was a pub a mile or so down the road which I was planning on visiting for dinner, but as I was heading back from my shower the clouds decided to open, and with it my hopes of a proper dinner vanished. No way was I going to get everything soaking wet right before bed and risk a cold wet night. Instead I grabbed at my fully stocked pannier, zipped myself up in the tent and scoffed away, updating the growing number of people who knew about my adventure on the days progress.

With friends and family updated (it's probably a bad sign that my absence from Facebook was being noticed) I was glad to put my phone on charge and get some sleep. I settled onto my back, then remembered that was a bad idea and moved to my side like I would at home on a proper mattress. Listening to the cars travelling down the motorway, I thought what a daft place for a campsite this was….and then I stopped thinking of anything.

Distance Travelled – 76 Miles
Hedgerows watered – 2 (13 Total)
Amazing tailwinds encountered – 1 (2 Total)

Campsite – 6/10 – Very well presented and up market looking site. But rather too close to the motorway and one of the more expensive ones I visited during the trip.

12 DAY 9, STRATHCLYDE TO ABERFELDY

After the traffic free and very easy to navigate previous day, today would be a massive culture shock as I'd no longer be following close to the M74, as that now veered off to the west towards Glasgow, whereas I'd now come across country enough. I'd spent a good hour the previous evening in the tent looking at various routes and I'd picked out as straight a line as possible to the north towards Inverness. I'd done my best to avoid as many built up areas as possible, but just couldn't escape the fact that the first few hours of this morning's cycle would see me navigating through the outer fringes of Glasgow. Luckily (or skilfully, take your pick) it was now Sunday, so as I left the campsite bright and early (well early anyway) and headed out onto the roads they were nice and quiet. The dry weather also allowed me to have my phone on the handlebars and my navigation app open, as I picked my way slowly through the streets of Bellshill and

Coatbridge.

Mercifully I seemed to be getting back out into the country as I left Coatbridge, after nearly an hour of cycling with one eye on the road and one on my map. The road may not have been a cyclists favourite, rather too twisty and narrow for that, but still being early on a Sunday it was manageable, and certainly preferable to staring at maps and street signs every two minutes. Besides, the further out of town I got, the better the road was getting, until it abruptly turned into a dual carriageway, the A73, as I neared Cumbernauld, and all hell broke loose.

Looking at the map now, with that wonderful thing hindsight, I could have turned off almost straight away and pretty much dodged Cumbernauld all together, passing to the east of it. But I didn't have the benefit of hindsight, and was fed up of staring at maps so I just ploughed on. It was very quiet and I knew there wasn't far to go until I could hang a right onto the A8011, which passed through the middle of the town. It didn't look very big on the map and the road was largely straight, plus it looked direct, so I didn't see it being a problem. Wrong. Wrong on many counts. Firstly the 'hang a right' part that I was planning was impossible, as the A8011 was a road which went right over the top of the dual carriageway I was currently on with no junction. Irritating. The only option now was to carry on for nearly another mile, navigate a few roundabouts, cross the M80, pick up the A8011 to the west, and then travel back across the M80 to end up, 2 miles later, on the bridge I'd just gone under. To rub salt into the wound the A8011 which had taken so much effort to reach, was also a terrible road, a dual carriageway that ploughed right through the middle of Cumbernauld. It was a bypass that didn't bypass. I don't mind saying that I was fairly pissy when I eventually made it out of the north side, clocking an impressive 25mph in doing so!

After a frustrating first couple hours to the day it felt great to be moving again, holding some good speed along the B816 until a very quick dash into a Spar, as I reluctantly left Bants locked up outside and feared for his safety in what looked less than a stand out area. Quick shop over and I was glad to wheel him off out of the way!

Bonnybridge came and went next at 22 miles into the day before I switched to the A872, which would take me the next 10 miles or so into the heart of Stirling. One reason for going straight through Stirling (other than it just being in the way) was that I wanted to pick up some more spare inner tubes, and a quick Google search had shown a Halfords which would be open on Sunday. As I cycled into Stirling I considered just carrying on, I did still have two spare tubes, but the thought of sitting by the side of the road in the middle of remote northern Scotland, with no spare tubes or patches, miles away from the nearest bike shop, brought me out in a cold sweat. With that in mind I made the 2 mile round detour to Halfords, picked up my tubes, and then picked up a burger from the burger van in the car park. Something for the bike, something for me I figured. More good news came when I spotted a proper cyclists track pump mounted outside the store, using that I was finally able to get some real pressure into my tyres for the first time since leaving home. Spare tubes and lots of pressure, no way am I going to get a puncture now!

With much greater peace of mind I left Stirling at 11:30am, headed through, and over Bridge of Allan and onto the B8033, which took me through Dunblane and back out into the beautiful quiet countryside, a real treat after a busy morning. However, by the time I reached the small village of Garrick on the A822 I was struggling. Struggling badly. It was only around 1:30pm but I felt absolutely done over, my legs had just gone like they hadn't done before. Every single turn of the pedals felt like torture and the worst problem was the hills, the ups and the downs. Obviously I expected to struggle on the uphill stretches, of which there were many today, but what I didn't expect was to struggle on the downhill parts too. I'd noticed a couple days earlier that if I stopped pedalling on a descent it was getting difficult to get moving again, the first few turns of the pedals were becoming painful until my legs accepted it and got on with it. But today they just wouldn't come back properly. It was taking minutes of turning the pedals through gritted teeth to get them moving again, and I couldn't keep them turning for that long, no sooner had I got them loosened up I was grinding to a halt on the next hill. Pulling over to the side of the road once more I stuffed some more food down me, not even caring what it was, and washed it down with an awful energy drink. Energy was needed.

After allowing myself five minutes I did manage to rally a little, willing myself to keep on going and finding something from somewhere. On through the busy town of Crieff where I gazed longingly at all the closed takeaways and shops right on the high street, where I daren't go in and leave Bants and all his panniers outside. I settled for stopping at a garage on the exit of town (partly because it seemed like a good excuse to stop pedalling up an endless hill) and did manage to find some nice fresh baguettes and fruit. Listening to my body seemed to be working okay so far, and it seemed to be craving fruit so I'd started grabbing it when I saw it…no offence to the Scots but that didn't seem too often in most shops I'd seen!

The 6 miles on from Crieff were hard going, and then it got truly ridiculous for a little while! It has to be said the scenery was truly indescribably stunning as the road wound its way through the hills (mountains!) but I was just too knackered to take much notice. What goes up must come down though and I finally got a reward for all my climbing with an incredible descent that raised my spirits.

With the afternoon drawing on I stopped to check my campsite options for the night. Few and far between said my phone. Aberfeldy seemed to be the only sensible option which would keep me on route, but that was another 12 miles away. On a good day that's not a problem but today I wasn't sure I had it in me. Letting out a sigh I reached for a Mars bar and got on with it. Nobody said this would be easy and it wasn't, the road was out to kill me, it just would not let up. Neither would the wind, it was blowing right into my face so that even when the road did level for a minute, I was still struggling along in first gear at walking pace. Then I decided walking was easier so I got off and did some more of that, then things deteriorated further and I'm pretty sure I was walking downhill at one point. This was only 12 miles but it felt like 1200, it just wouldn't end. Every time I looked at the distance on the phone it seemed to have moved an impossibly small amount, I half expected it to start increasing.

6 miles still to go and the temptation to just throw the tent up at the side of the road was immense. I was done. Nothing left. Nothing in the tank, no second wind (or ninth wind), one broken cyclist, come and have a look folks. Then the road did let up, it levelled out. Then it started sloping downhill enough that I could actually roll. Then I began rolling fast enough that I needed to do some braking, I'd honestly never been so happy to find a hill in my life. Barely dropping 20mph, I covered the last 5 miles down into Aberfeldy before rolling right on through town to the campsite on the outskirts. I had arrived! It was only around 5:30pm but it felt like midnight and I was so pleased to be able to get off the bike and get my tent up. I just wanted to stop.

On my trip through Aberfeldy there was one shop I did want to visit though, so after setting up the tent and filling it with supplies, I reluctantly jumped back on Bants for the short trip into town, returning ten minutes later with a huge portion of fish and chips.

Perfection. I zipped myself up in the tent and greedily ate, stretching my aching legs out as I did so. Fish and chips honestly never tasted so good.

Dinner complete and there some problems to solve. Tomorrows route looked problematic at best, there just weren't enough roads no matter how long I stared at the map on my phone. In sheer desperation I got out my backup paper map which didn't help at all, I'm not sure why I thought it would really, it's not like it would have an extra road on it just for me. After staring at the maps for far too long I decided what I really wanted to do was head northwest from Aberfeldy, join the A9 and follow that to Inverness. It looked reasonably direct but my concern was that the A9 would be a busy dual carriageway, and although there seemed to be a few sections where it would be possible to use adjoining roads, this wasn't the case the whole way. I really didn't want to kill myself. My other option was to head through the middle of Cairngorms National Park before making my way west to Inverness. This route had the positive of avoiding any major roads, but at the expense of being far longer and most likely taking in many more hills. 'Be safe!' said my friend, to which I replied I was trying, but I was tired and it looked like so much further! I then had the brainwave of getting Mum to have a look at the sections of A9 I couldn't avoid, using Google Streetview on her computer! Genius! A short while later Mum confirmed that the A9 did indeed look like a very busy dual carriageway, but that she spotted what looked like a cycle route sign beside it. Of course! If there's one thing I was learning the last few days, it was that the Scots loved their cycle tracks, and following a quick bit of research we found there was a cycle route sticking close to the A9 which led all the way to Inverness. Amazing news. With my route now sorted I was a much happier camper as I settled down for another broken nights sleep in my tent. It felt colder than the previous night, so I was wearing everything when I pulled my sleeping bag over me and it seemed to do the trick as I didn't wake through coldness, just being uncomfortable or worrying about various things! On the positive side however, another day down, another day closer to the finish. Come on now, keep it up.

Distance Travelled – 75 Miles
Hedgerows watered – 1 (14 Total)
Utter desperation moments at Scotland's hills – 3

Campsite – 6/10 – Not a bad campsite, situated on the edge of town in a stunning part of Scotland. Very friendly staff with okay facilities, although a bit of paint in the bare brickwork toilets wouldn't go amiss. Not sure why pitches needed to be allocated to tents when there were only ever going to be a couple at this time of year, would have been nice to have spread out a little and found an area slightly less muddy. That said, very happy to have found this open campsite.

13 DAY 10, ABERFELDY TO INVERNESS

'Oh my god you look like death' was the lovely message I received after sending a selfie from the campsite early on day 10. Zooming in on the photo I had to agree, I looked terrible. Going to the toilets and having a wash and brushing my teeth did nothing to improve matters…..nope, still look like death Ross.

Despite my appearance I did feel reasonably okay and being packed up and on the road before 8am was a morale booster. The first 5 miles or so went reasonably smoothly, including me having a giggle as I passed through a place called 'Dull'. In a stroke of sheer genius the village had been twinned with somewhere called 'Boring' in Oregan. I was tempted to stop for a picture but I was flying downhill at the time and didn't feel like stopping. As it happened my friend Tim had passed through in his campervan earlier in the year, and when I told him about the place he produced a photo he'd stopped to take! I've since also learnt that the places of Dull and Boring have now teamed up with the county of 'Bland' in Australia which is just amazing. I now want to visit all three just to say I have.

Not long after Dull and the hills started in earnest, leaving me doing rather more pushing than I'd have liked along the B846. So slow was my progress than even after an acceptable start it still took a couple hours to cover the 15 miles to Tummel Bridge. Then things got really bad. The road began zig zagging up and down, the hills far too steep to just go straight over. I climbed hundreds of metres, well pushed more accurately, only to then have to lose all that hard earned height and have to start all over again. The campsite had been at 140 metres above sea level, and I'd simply lost track of the amount of times I'd climbed to well over 400 metres and then back down again, the ride profile for this section will look like a heart attack I thought to myself. To further my misery rain also began to fall, not even a stunning downhill section on the approach to the A9 could lift my spirits. Spotting the cycle track alongside did cheer me up slightly although when I stopped to check my progress, or lack of, it made worrying reading. I'd been travelling for four hours and had only managed 25 miles. This was painfully slow. When I'd crossed into Scotland a few days earlier I was so happy to have a whole week to finish the trip to John O'Groats, feeling absolutely certain that it would be plenty of time. But now I wasn't so sure. It wouldn't be at this rate.

More bad news came when I began heading along the 'cycle path'. I'd been well and truly spoilt by some of the excellent cycle paths I'd encountered in Scotland so far, as such I was expecting good things from one of the main routes through the country. No. Being incredibly thankful that I'd stopped for spare inner tubes, I spent the next 5 miles bouncing my way along a rough, bumpy, gravelled mess of a route. One minute I was pressed up to the far side of the Armco against the side of the A9, bouncing through overgrown bushes as I went, the next I was having to drop down away from the road, pass through deep gravel, dodge large rocks, holes and poor bridges. It was a nightmare and a completely unsuitable place to be on a road bike, this was proper mountain bike territory. All this coupled with my already slow start to the day, and the wind doing its best to stop me going anywhere, led me to the belief that Scotland might be beating me.

Despite my worsening mood I did manage a smile when I spotted a sign declaring this to be the 'Highest Point on the Cycling Network.' Good, I thought, I don't have much more left in me. As it turned out this was the turning point, quite literally in fact as the road had now curved around a large hill and was heading north. All of a sudden I seemed to have a tail wind, instead of the surrounding valleys channelling it right at me as they had been. Throwing caution to the wind I went for it and was having immense fun, bouncing and sliding my way precariously through the gravel on my skinny tyres. With the wind behind me I was moving again and it felt great. It felt even better when the cycle path switched to the virtually unused A889 another 5 miles later.

Stopping at a quiet garage in Dalwhinne, I leaned Bants up against the wall next to the deserted forecourt and went into the shop to be confronted by seven or eight Chinese girls crowded into the small area. This was very confusing as there was a complete lack of cars outside, so I'd no idea where they'd come from, quite frankly they looked confused as well so I took the opportunity to nab the last sandwich and a handful of snacks, pay the equally confused looking guy behind the counter and get out of there. Checking around when I left revealed that there were definitely no cars around, how bizarre.

Everything that had been wrong during the morning was now right, I pondered to myself as I sped away from Dalwhinne. The weather was now dry and bright, the road was smooth, quiet, suitable, and while certainly not flat it was at least manageable. Plus that tail wind, that beautiful beautiful tail wind that felt like a friend giving you a reassuring pat on the back as it pushed you on, making you go faster and giving you more energy in the process. The 12 miles to Newtonmore flew by in a blur, taking far less than an hour, so I decided to stop at a Spar for some more celebratory food. All that struggling during the morning may have been slow going, but it certainly worked up an appetite.

Second lunch over and I was off again, flying 20 miles up the wonderful B970 to Aviemore. This road did stray a little further from the A9 than was strictly necessary, and I almost stuck with another B road that did cling closely to the A9, but with hindsight I made the right decision and enjoyed a wonderfully speedy and isolated 20 miles, stopping just once to snap some photos beside Ruthven Castle. Well strictly speaking Ruthven Barracks, which had been built on the site of the old castle in 1715. (I may have searched it on Google later on that night) Either way it was an impressive sight and I wished, not for the first time on this trip, that I had a little more time available to go and investigate.

Passing through Aviemore and I stuck to the signed cycle route I'd been with since finding the A9 earlier, but it now did its favourite trick and once more went from the sublime to the ridiculous. Leaving Aviemore via a quiet housing estate, I soon found myself on a wide relatively firm gravel path, which then turned into a loose gravel path that led me out through some trees before spending several miles winding me through the countryside. I eventually found myself with mountain bikers for company, as I emerged through rutted bumpy tracks into a place called Boat Of Garten. Not for the first time I wondered what on earth people were thinking with these cycle routes. I'm all for there being as many cycle ways as possible, and for them to be off road as much as possible, but if you're going to call something a 'National Cycle Network' then there needs to be some consistency to it. You can't have beautiful freshly laid tarmac one minute, with signage, mile markers and handily painted sections, before two miles later resorting to a dodgy path through a forest.

At the very least it needs to be made clear which tracks are suitable for road bikes, especially tourers, and which are only of any use if you're riding a mountain bike, preferably fitted with suspension. At any rate with all confidence now lost in the cycle routes I vowed to just go back to choosing my own routes, it had worked well before and that's what I would do for the final part of the trip.

Back on some firm tarmac I pulled over in Boat of Garten to try and figure out where to stay that night. I'd already searched for a campsite earlier on but my phone was struggling for signal in the forest, now back in a town I could pull up Google and search again. The results were not good. It was already gone 4pm and I was feeling relatively tired. The morning, despite getting absolutely nowhere, had been hard work, and I'd been pushing hard all afternoon to try and make up time. Ideally I was after a campsite just outside Boat of Garten but there was literally nothing. The closest available without resorting to going wildly off course was Auchnahillin Holiday Park, but that was nearly in Inverness, some 22 miles further on. It was right on course though. Ringing them up I rather hoped they'd be shut for the season, but they were open, so with a weary sigh I resigned myself to another 22 miles…once I'd eaten another Mars bar of course, desperate times call for desperate measures!

Covering the first half of the journey to the campsite was very easy going, much to my relief, but that didn't last as I started struggling on the hills and losing the wind assistance I'd been having all afternoon. 'Noooo' I pleaded to the skies, just help me out a little longer. They did, I dealt with a particularly hilly section before the roads and the winds were kind to me once more, helping me to Auchnahillin Holiday Park in just under two hours, good progress at the end of a long day. It's just as well progress had been good as I realised my front light had packed up at some point during the previous few days. Luckily I arrived with the last of the daylight just after 6pm, the quiet roads also helping, but if it had gotten any later I could have been in trouble, or cycling via the light from the led on my phone!

As I'd been told on the phone earlier, the sites reception was closed, so I picked myself out a quiet spot in the corner of the small site and set up for the night. A quick look around showed me the site had a small kitchen and library area, but all I was really after was a hot shower.

Shower found and I was soon clean, dry, and back in my tent and pondering what a strange day it had been. The first half had been absolutely desperate and left me at my lowest since the soaking in Cornwall all the way back on day one. But the afternoon had been mega, sure the effort had taken it out of me, but as I sat munching through my supplies I was incredibly proud to have dug deep and turned what could have been a near write off of a day into such a positive one, covering nearly 100 miles. As I studied the map I could see I was only around 10 miles outside of Inverness, the last 'big place' I'd need to navigate. From worrying about running out of time I was now certain I had plenty of it, I could maybe even manage it in two days from here! No, don't get over excited, small achievable targets, that's what worked well for me I'd come to realise and part of the reason I'd gotten on such a downer this morning. I'd been looking at the trip from the campsite to the A9 as a 'short spurt' before I started the day properly, when in actual fact it was 25 miles. That would have been bad enough but combined with the poor weather and hills it had nearly broken me. Okay then, three achievable days I told myself, even that would still leave me a couple days spare. Just take it steady, nearly there. Don't do anything silly now, especially not this close to Inverness, the thought of ending back in the same hospital I'd been in three months earlier filled me with dread. Surely the embarrassment of that would kill me on its own.

Finally finished with my food, maps, planning and excited conversations for the night, I settled down for some well-earned rest. Nearly there…

Distance Travelled – 94 Miles
Hedgerows watered – 2 (16 Total)
Utter desperation moments at Scotland's hills – Far too many to count (Rising Total)
Amazing tailwinds encountered – 1 (3 Total)

Campsite – 8/10 – I really liked this campsite. Situated on a quiet road in a stunning location, it isn't glitzy or posh but is was well maintained and charming while offering good value for money. One to visit.

14 DAY 11, INVERNESS TO LAIRGE

Unzipping the tent first thing in the morning was always a cause for excitement, as you gazed at the sky for the first time to see what sort of weather you had to start the day with. This morning it was stunning. Excellent. With a smile on my face I got ready for the days adventure with a spring in my step, I definitely felt good today, anything was possible.

Ready to leave and the sites reception was still closed, but finding a message book and a list of tariffs in a bag on the door handle, I left the right money and a note in their book, signed 'the mad cyclist.' A glance in any mirror revealed that I really was starting to look like a mad adventurer by this point. That or a homeless man, I couldn't really decide.

The first part of the days journey involved a long downhill stretch towards Inverness, which left my hands frozen to the brake levers. Picking my way through a housing estate near the city, I spotted a Co-op so I stopped to pick up something for breakfast and to give my hands a chance to thaw out. Win win.

As I ate my breakfast and the feeling returned to my fingers, I again checked the route on my phone as the next part looked like it had potential to go wrong. Ultimately I knew I had to find my way to the Kessock Bridge, a large cable-stayed bridge which carried the A9 across the Beauly Firth. I imagined it must have a cycle path or pavement on at least one side of it, if not I'd solve that problem when I got to it.

With breakfast finished I continued my way down towards the river, nearly missing a few turns on the way but just about avoiding any mistakes. Picking up the A96 and a handy cycle track took me to the A9, which featured another cycle path alongside. This now brought me perilously close to Raigmore hospital which I'd seen rather too much of on my last visit to Inverness!

Being very careful I followed the A9, past Inverness Football Club and onto the impressive Kessock Bridge. That was easy! Stopping halfway along the bridge to have a look over the side was a mistake, it was surprisingly high and windy and I'm not great with heights at the best of times. Carrying on I kept my eyes staring dead forward until I made it back onto solid ground.

Once over the bridge I thought the last part of my tricky navigation was behind me, but was soon met with a sign saying that the cycle path was closed. Feeling rather irritated I followed the diversion signs, which took me across the dual carriageway (not easy!) and down a small road. A small road that was getting smaller by the minute as I dropped down a large hill and around a corner, before climbing back up again and past a final few driveways until the road just turned into a driveway for the final house. Flicking my phone on did nothing to improve matters as my navigation app had stopped working. Talk about perfect timing! In fairness it had been working remarkably well for the whole trip, but I think recording my route for 10 days straight had been an error. It would have been better to have split the recordings into days instead of resuming each morning. Still, the occasional problem was normally solved by restarting the app and the data didn't seem to get lost, today however even restarting wasn't solving the issue and to further my annoyance I couldn't even get enough data to load a map. Ideas of getting my paper map out were quickly dismissed, as I realised the tiny roads I was looking for just wouldn't be on there.

Running out of ideas I turned around from this obvious dead end and headed back the way I'd come, only this time spotting another diversion sign I'd missed which pointed down a path. Aha! The path soon became too rough to cycle so I started pushing as me and Bants bumped along. As the path continued it just got worse and it was a struggle to push Bants, his wheels sinking into the mud as we climbed up and then down under the trees. This was without doubt a stupid place to be trying to take a bike I thought to myself as I ground to a halt, feet slipping in the mud. All I needed was a road, literally any road. Off to my right through the trees I could just make out the back of some houses which looked out over the river, but there were no gaps through to them and what can only be described as a small cliff stood in the way on my left. Behind me was one dead end road and the dual carriageway A9 which was apparently unpassable, the only choice was to press on.

Pressing on was getting harder and harder though, but eventually I emerged through what appeared to be someone's back garden and down a driveway onto a small lane. At least if there's a driveway there must be some way of getting to a main road I thought, but after cycling back and forth a little I couldn't see it. What I'd taken to be the way out turned out to be another driveway. Giving serious thought to the fact that I was never going to get out of this place I finally spotted a pleasant looking couple coming out of a house I'd just passed. Approaching them in sheer desperation I think my first words were 'How do I get out of here?!?' before I backtracked slightly and explained how I'd ended up quite so badly lost, much to their amusement. We decided that somebody must have been messing around with the diversion signs, before they pointed me back down the lane and around a small corner, following this took me right along the waterfront all the way back to the end of the Kessock Bridge where I'd been diverted. Except now I was on a small lane under it and no better off, just half an hour later. It may have been idyllic here on the front in the sunshine, but I really just wanted to crack on, all this wasted time and effort wasn't getting me any closer to John O'Groats.

By the time I'd negotiated North Kessock and found my way up to Tore and back onto the A9, I was feeling very grumpy. It had taken an hour and twenty minutes to cover what would have been 4 miles from the bridge to this point on the A9. Plus so much effort, and mud. Trying to put that behind me I continued along the A9 which was now no longer a dual carriageway, but instead a very fast moving single road. Speeding along and doing my best to ignore the cars and lorries thundering past me, I headed downhill towards the Cromarty Bridge, giving a wave to a couple of other cycle tourers who were coming in the opposite direction. Part of me envied them touring as a pair, sometimes I felt it would have been nice to have someone to share the experiences with, or to have dinner with at night. But on the flip side I could go as fast or slow as I pleased, in any direction I so wished and stop when and where I liked. Nobody to answer to. There are undoubtedly a lot of positive and negative aspects to both options and I'd like to try out a pair, or even group ride at some point in the future for comparison.

After crossing the Cromarty Bridge I persevered with the A9 for only a few more miles before deciding that somebody was going to hit me at some point before John O'Groats on this road. Now that I was on it large parts of it were coming back to me too from when I'd driven up here in June, so I knew that it didn't get much better. Instead I pressed my backup plan into action and turned off at Evanton, joining the B9176 which would take me north towards Bonnar Bridge, before I carried on through the centre of northern Scotland up to the coast, finishing with a quick (optimism!) sprint east to John O'Groats. If you say it fast enough it really does sound easy. The obvious down side to this route was the extra mileage, but I felt so much happier and safer once back on the quiet country roads that this more than made up for it. In fact I was so happy that I pulled over to send a couple texts to say that I was being sensible and that I planned on coming home very much alive. It was now gone 12 and having only made it to the other side of Inverness, I quickly ate some food and set about covering some ground.

Bonnar Bridge was my next target at 20 miles away and the quiet roads and good mood aided my progress. The final few miles into Bonnar Bridge were a wonderful descent down the A836 through Ardchronie and Kincardine. I'd stopped before this and fitted my small video camera to the handlebars, catching some great footage that will jog my memory of the trip for years to come.

As food had been hard to come by all day, I stopped for some when the opportunity arose in Bonnar Bridge. Whilst eating I began checking out campsite options for the night but as it was still reasonably early I made sure to look slightly further ahead than normal. Despite the large search area results were still minimal though, this really was rural northern Scotland now! One option which did appear to be fairly close to my route was Poolside Camping, but this was only just past Lairge, a mere 14 miles further on. Without any other possibilities I decided to head towards this one for the moment, but to perhaps try another search once I was closer as stopping in 14 miles time would make this one of the shortest days of the trip.

Once back on Bants and travelling north on the A386, it soon became clear that I'd be spending the night at Poolside camping. The further I pedaled, the more the skies darkened until eventually it began raining as I cycled through Lairge. Stopping under the shelter of a tree I grabbed the waterproof case for my phone out of my bag and safely tucked the phone inside. Being only a few miles from the campsite I was in a rush to get there before the really heavy rain showed up, plus despite still being early it was getting towards the stage where lights would soon be needed. Cycling along the quiet road I held my waterproofed phone to the side of the bars, this allowed me to make sure I didn't miss the turning I was after. Needn't have worried as it turned out, roads in this area were few and far between!

After turning off and following a small road around the edge of a field, I found a house which looked like any other perfectly normal house in the country, but according to the map this should be the campsite. For some reason I hadn't rung ahead as usual, probably as I was expecting to cycle on and find somewhere further down the road, so I hoped they weren't shut for the season. Finally spotting a small camping sign in the front garden improved my hopes as the weather continued to deteriorate, judging by the muddy driveway I was struggling to push Bants along it must have been raining here for some time.

The driveway took me around to the back of the house but it wasn't very clear where to go next, at least the small field featured a static caravan and a water post in the centre so I knew I was on the campsite, the question was just if they were actually open or not. Approaching the back of the house I knocked on the door and did find somebody who told me to go ahead and set up where I liked. Relief! My host pointed out the toilets, showers, and small rec room before he went off to find me some change. As it looked like being a rough night I pitched my tent on the highest ground I could find, which was also conveniently close to the rec room. After unloading Bants he was wheeled into the room out of the elements while I spied some plug sockets, getting very excited about the prospect of charging my batteries. After digging them out though I discovered the sockets didn't work which was a shame, but I reasoned I had enough charge for the moment and didn't need to go knocking at the house again. Besides Bants, the rec room contained a pool table, some books, a bar area and a very comfy looking old sofa, in fact if you squinted hard enough it looked like the basement set from any number of 1990's teen TV shows. Not a bad thing by the way!

Tent set up and Bants hidden away, I squelched my way through the mud to the toilets and showers.

These were a little different to anything else I'd encountered on the trip, perhaps it would be kindest to just say they were a little more wooden and primitive looking than usual and leave it there. They were clean however and there was hot water which did the job. Functional at least, say no more.

Back in the tent for yet another makeshift dinner and I wondered how many more of these I'd have to suffer? That was a good question. As I sat gazing at the map, me and the inside of the tent dimly lit by my phone as the wind picked up outside, I realised I was only 99 miles from John O'Groats. 99 miles. Double digits. A wave of excitement washed over me that this could be all over by this time tomorrow. Then I really thought about it. 99 miles, when was the last time I'd covered 99 miles in one day? Ages, that's how long, sure I'd come close a few times but what were the chances of managing it on day 12. Slim, that was the chance. No, I forcefully told myself, you've still got 4 whole days to do this, there's no rush, this can be like a victory lap, a couple of short days on the bike before a couple more days relaxing and then home. Every time you've set a big target it's gone wrong and you've depressed yourself, listen to yourself for once and take your time. I was talking sense, the trouble is I rarely listen to myself. That said, as I laid down, listening to the wind howl and the rain beat against the tent, I promised to at least try this time. There's no rush, all you'll achieve is another day kicking your heels with nothing to do, while you wait to come home. Listen for once Ross, listen.

Distance Travelled – 65 Miles
Hedgerows Watered – 3 (19 Total)

Campsite – 5/10 – Apologies to this small family run campsite but despite having a certain charm in some ways it was the worst of the trip. The muddy flooded driveway I had to push Bants through didn't help, and neither did having to wander around like a lost sheep looking for some form of reception. The people were lovely and the small 'rec room' is a nice idea, however the toilets and showers are a bit 'primitive', not great.

15 DAY 12, LAIRGE TO JOHN O'GROATS

I've had some rubbish nights sleep in my life but none will ever compare to the night spent in my tent at Poolside Campsite. The wind was just indescribable, every time I so much as managed to start dozing then a huge gust would catch the tent so fiercely, that the roof would be blown over to nearly the ground on the far side of the tent, whacking the side of the tent into me in the process. The rain meanwhile, while easing off as the morning crept into sight, was torrential during the early hours. I'd never had so little sleep. Finally calling it a day at 5:30am, I sat up and decided to make an early start to the day, laying here was doing me no good at all. My only problem was just how to get up. In my quest to save weight and space on the packing, I didn't have any tent pegs or guy ropes with me, in truth I hardly ever use them anyway, instead relying on all the items in my tent to keep it from blowing away. But in this weather that was never going to be enough and I didn't really want to stand outside in the rain trying to pack everything from the tent onto the bike, while stopping the tent itself blowing away. The temptation to just leave everything where it was and make a mad dash for John O'Groats and the finish line was immense. No Ross you can't do that, I told myself. Or can I? No, no absolutely not.

Getting out of the tent I had a brainwave and simply dragged the whole thing, contents and all, across the slick grass, wedging it half into the door way of the rec room where Bants had spent a dry night. I looked at the inviting sofa in the corner and wondered why I hadn't just stayed here, nobody would have minded. Packing up in the dry was always so much easier, even if folding up the cold soaking wet tent and persuading it into its bag was still a miserable job.

All packed up and ready to go and I had a peek outside. Good news was the rain had all but stopped, bad news was that it was still fairly dark and I hadn't fixed my front light. Staring into the darkness for a few seconds allowed my eyes to adjust and I figured I could manage like it until the sun came up. The roads here were utterly deserted, open for miles around and my rear light was working. Wheeling Bants out, I shut the rec room door behind me and squelched my way down the muddy waterlogged driveway, before encountering some tarmac and getting underway, utterly determined to make it to John O'Groats today. I'd had enough of this, I just wanted it done and done now, so I got my head down, squinted into the darkness and got on with it.

Out onto the A836 and Scotland had saved me the best till last. Sure visibility may have been slightly poor but that would soon change as the weather cleared, the sun rose over the hills and the wind pushed me along a beautifully empty single track road through stunning Scotland, towards the finish line. Bliss. Utter bliss. It seemed there was nobody else in the world as mile after mile of sheer perfection passed me by in serene silence, the only noise the gentle whirring from Bants as we powered on with all manner of wildlife jumping out of our way. Rabbits, sheep, deer, it seems they'd all come out to say hello.

With 20 miles covered I turned onto the B873, a cheeky looking shortcut I'd spotted from the national cycle network road I'd ended up on. My new road hugged the edge of Loch Naver for 6 miles before turning north and following the River Naver. By now I'd completely forgotten my previous favourite road in the Lake District, this was my new cycling nirvana and I'd give anything to have it as part of my local rideout. Especially if it could be arranged that the incredible tailwind be present at all times! I was barely out of top gear all morning, speeding along like I'd gotten excited and started racing someone on a Sunday Sportive. The thought of John O'Groats and the finish seemed to have given me endless energy, despite a complete lack of any meaningful sleep the previous night.

Despite stopping a number of times to take photos (mostly as each time I thought I'd found the most beautiful place to take a photo, I'd round the next corner and find somewhere even better) I'd still re-joined the A836 and made it to the northern coast of Scotland in comfortably under four hours. Bettyhill (aptly named) was the first place I'd seen all day which had a shop of sorts, in fact it was the first place I'd seen all day that had more than two houses! After a great 44 miles I was eager to get some lunch, and popped into the small general stores / post office to see what I could find.

The past, that's what I found. Although you'll no doubt by now have realised I'm far from a city dweller, I am reasonably modern and even though I'd spent a few days in more rural areas by this point, the small shops never failed to surprise and delight me. Due to the remoteness and sheer lack of people, one shop often has to serve many purposes, as do the people. So, in this case, I walked in to a shop to find a Postman collecting papers and other supplies to drop off to his customers, really can't imagine doing that back at home. As well as being a post office this shop was also doubling up as a supermarket, a café, and a general community meeting place. I marvelled at how wonderful it all was as I ate my egg mayonnaise sandwich and cakes, this really was like another world sometimes.

Moving on from Bettyhill and the scenery along the north coast was stunning, it reminded me of being back home in Devon, which I soon would be! In my head this was now nothing more than a quick dart along the coast to the finish line, but all too soon a signpost greeted me with the news that I still had nearly 50 miles to go before reaching John O'Groats. I'd got excited too soon again. Progress slowed a little as I had to climb a few hills, plus the wind was becoming a little more unpredictable and kept catching me from the side and getting me into wobbles…no accidents now please!

Onwards, onwards through tiny village after tiny village. The lack of any meaningful sized places had given me a lack of smaller targets to aim for, so I just kept my head down and kept plugging on, but I was feeling it now, 12 days on the bike with so little preparation was taking its toll and I was flagging. Come on, come on, a little further I thought as I passed through another nameless village.

My phone buzzed a few times. 'Are you there yet?' asked in several ways by text and by phone calls. I was glad so few people knew I was on the finishing stretch, that I was here at all. To quote the legendary Guy Martin, I was 'blowing out my arse' and hanging on as best I could, I didn't need to keep explaining that I hadn't arrived just yet. This was still nearly a 100 mile day on day 12, it wasn't going to happen in an instant as much as I'd have liked it to.

Ignoring the John O'Groats signs as much as possible, I'd instead been aiming for Thurso, a much more achievable sounding 20 miles closer to me. But as I closed in on this familiar place, on a long fast downhill stretch, Bants let out a high pitched scream. You can laugh and say objects don't scream but he did.

I tensed and started squeezing the brakes harder, wanting to stop but not wanting to put any more stress through the bike, as I waited for something to fall off or the back wheel to lock up. With the hill being so steep, stopping was proving to be an issue, and it wasn't until the road levelled out that I was finally able to manage it. Glancing down at the rear wheel nothing looked immediately amiss. I wondered if the rear hub was failing, it had been such a sudden and prominent noise, not something that had started quietly and gotten worse over time. 30 miles Bants, don't let me down now mate I pleaded, reaching into a pannier for some oil. While holding the back of the bike off the ground and spinning the rear wheel, I listened carefully but everything sounded okay. Perhaps it was the weight on a damaged hub making all that noise I mused? Throwing some oil at it seemed like a desperate throw of the dice before getting back on and moving off once more. Moving off rather slowly.

I covered a gentle mile with no issues until again that familiar noise started. Riding along the flat this time I leaned the bike from side to side, finding that I could alter the noise and even stop it. Hmm. Stopping once more I leant Bants up against a wall and walked around him, before this time immediately spotting the glaringly obvious problem. Due to the placement of the panniers and tent, I'd had to make a large bracket to mount my rear light much further back, as it just got completely hidden when mounted to the back of the rack itself. My bracket and light had now spent over 900 miles bouncing up and down, until they had finally fractured the end of the aluminium pannier rack on one side, this had allowed one side of my bracket to drop and catch on the tyre, making the noise. It wasn't until I'd walked right around the back of the bike that I'd seen it, the panniers and tent hiding the bracket from the side.

Immensely relieved that Bants wasn't going to give up on me just before the finish, I had renewed energy to push on through Thurso. Familiar places! It was now less than 20 miles to the finish. 20 miles. I started recognising buildings and landmarks from the trip here in the camper van after my crash last time, and knew I'd soon be closing in on the actual piece of road I'd crashed on. Slowing, not wanting to miss it, I started looking to the sides of the road and into the distance before eventually I found it.

Stopping beside the road I checked my phone, 8 miles from John O'Groats. It was crazy to think of all the preparation and effort that had gone into the first attempt only for it to end here, with me laying on this piece of road under this bike after 8 miles. Yet now here I was again, 3 months and 12 days later, having struggled to get back moving again, to get back to work, and finally to cover over 900 miles to be here. I could barely believe it was happening. Shaking my head I carried on, the blue skies seemed to be here just for me as I gingerly made my way closer. 7 miles. 6. 5. This is going to happen. 4. 3. What will happen when I get there? 2. In the distance I could see the car park, toilets and small café which sat beside the sign, the campsite opposite and then finally, appearing from behind the building, the sign, as always with a few people stood beside posing for photos. Eyes back on the road for the left turn down towards the car park, roll down the hill, careful through the carpark, really don't want to get knocked off now. Into first gear and carefully around the café, before one final push of the pedals takes me up the slope and alongside the famous sign.

Looking out to sea, I pulled a water bottle from the frame and had a long drink. I'd arrived. I stared for a moment, unsure what to do next. Being so fixated on getting here it felt very odd to have actually managed it, and I suddenly felt like all my focus was gone. What next? As I was pondering this, the couple who I'd seen snapping photos at the sign on my way in, approached me to ask if I'd come from Land's End and if I'd like my picture taken. Yes and yes please.

Pictures taken and stories swapped, I made sure to wait until they'd disappeared out of view before checking the photos to make sure I was actually in them, I needed evidence of this! Thankfully there were several good shots amongst the bunch so thanks very much random strangers. Just as I was thinking about all different people I'd met over the past 12 days, I was approached by another cyclist who had arrived just half an hour before me, having also completed the Land's End to John O'Groats. See, not the only one silly enough to attempt it in October after all. As we swapped stories it became clear we'd used wildly different routes, and wildly different bikes by the looks of it although that was to be expected, my little road bike wouldn't be many peoples first choice for a long tour. But that's the great thing about these tours and what was being demonstrated to me now, you can do them any number of ways on any number of machines in any amount of time. No matter how you do it you'll have had an adventure, and what an adventure it was.

Distance Travelled – 94 Miles
Hedgerows watered – 1 (20 Total)
Amazing tailwinds encountered – 1 (4 Total)
Challenges crossed off bucket list – 1!
Total Distance from Land's End to John O'Groats – 961 Miles

16 WHAT NEXT?

Having read the end of that last chapter back a few times, I can't help but think it feels rather anti-climactic. Rewriting it hasn't helped. The only conclusion and explanation I can offer you, is that it sounds anti-climactic, because the event itself was. There is just no escaping that. It was a solo adventure. A solo adventure that finished nearly a thousand miles away from home, hence I was never going to be met by friends or family at the finish line. Also, being a solo adventure, as opposed to some form of organised event as I'm used to, meant there would be no fanfare provided. Even at the end of a local Sunday Sportive, riders will cross under a finish line, usually whilst being announced over a PA system, and enter into an area filled with other cyclists and friends. You'll then receive either a small trophy or t-shirt, certainly some form of memento to remember the day. At the other extreme when I used to race cars, you'd cross the finish line, flashing under a waving chequered flag at over 100mph, before completing a slow in lap in front of the crowd, waving to the marshals as you did so. Then entering into a parc-ferme area, there would be officials as well as your mechanics and your other competitors, all swapping stories of their race. If you were really lucky you'd then get to visit the podium, collect a trophy in front of the crowd, and maybe even spray some champagne. By contrast, rolling up to a signpost at the tip of Scotland on your own and saying, 'Yes, that's that done then' was never going to compare! As far as most people knew, I could have come from 10 miles down the road.

Since arriving home, I've spoken to a lot of people who have had similar experiences at the end of a long solo challenge. You become so fixated on just getting through the challenge, that once it's over you suddenly feel rather lost. For 12 days I had been struggling onwards to the finish in the same routine. Wake up, pack up, cycle as hard and as fast as possible for as long as possible, find food, find somewhere to stay, plan the next day, sleep. Over and over again. Now it was over. My overpowering emotion was one of relief. I'd done it. The only question was what to do next?

It was now 4pm on Wednesday 11th October 2017. As it would soon be getting dark, I needed to stop milling around a sign post at the edge of the sea and find somewhere to stay for the night! After spending 10 of the previous 13 nights in a tent, it was time for a slight upgrade, in the form of a glamping style pod at Bower Wigwams. Yes they're called wigwams but they really didn't look like it. However they were rather beautiful wooden huts, equipped with electricity, heaters, TV, and thick enough foam that almost passed as a bed. Alongside the small collection of 'wigwams' was a modern kitchen / dining room, as well as toilet and shower. With Bants locked to the front of my room for the night, and my tent wonderfully still packed up, I had a shower before eating dinner in the communal kitchen with a wonderful German couple who were hiking parts of Scotland. This trip really did throw up some interesting people, I thought to myself as I walked back to my wigwam. Feeling the wonderful heat upon opening the door, and not having to worry about starting the next day cold, or wet, I did wonder why I'd been so insistent on using my tent for the entire trip. I knew the answer, trying to be a hero. Plus camping is great as long as you're not cold and wet!

Safely tucked up in the wigwam, and I had a real moment of acceptance at what I'd just achieved. Plus the added bonus of covering 13 miles to reach Bower Wigwams was an increase in the last days total mileage to 107, making it the longest day of the trip. That felt like something to be proud of as I drifted off to some well-earned sleep.

17 ORKNEY!

Well there's a crazy idea, why not! Given that my train and car hire weren't booked until Saturday, I still had Thursday and Friday to kill, and as beautiful as northern Scotland is, there isn't a great deal to do. With this in mind, I decided to catch the ferry over to Orkney to see what it had to offer. Plus what were the chances I'd ever get to do this again? So, a 10 mile early morning cycle took me to Gills Bay, just west of John O'Groats, to catch the ferry to Orkney. Due to it being off season, the smaller passenger only ferry wasn't running, meaning I'd instead use the larger car ferry. This was even larger than expected, a huge Catamaran capable of carrying 9 articulated Lorries, 30 cars and hundreds of passengers.

We didn't have quite that many people on board as we made the hour long crossing to St.Margarets Hope, enjoying stunning views of Orkney and Caithness in the process. Well, most of the other passengers were enjoying the views, personally I was just trying not to be sick, something I'm very happy to say I managed, even if I was looking slightly pale as I wheeled Bants down the ramp, and onto solid ground. Beautiful firm, non-rocking, solid ground!

Feeling slightly better, I had a look around St.Margarets Hope before setting off for the southern tip of the island. One thing that did take me by surprise were the winds, they were just impossible and travelling the few miles to the southern tip took an absolute age. Once there I did however meet a chap whilst exploring a Neolithic tomb, who had cycled across America, the next large cycling related item on my bucket list. Small world. Once we'd finished swapping stories of our trips, I set off back to that nights campsite, which was another glamping site of sorts. Whelan Farm Campsite, without doubt the most wonderfully strange place I have ever, or will ever, stay in my life. The wooden 'pods' were far simpler than the ones on the mainland the previous night, they were however still dry and warm, perfectly acceptable. It was the rest of the site where things got strange. Very strange, like being in some weird cross over episode of 'Father Ted' and 'Carry on Camping.' The kitchen and laundrette areas had seen far better days, but still had an amazing charm, with handwritten notes attached to everything. Polite notices about 'fresh towels being provided' sat next to a rusty old washing machine and a window so grime covered you could barely see out if it. The whole place was one extreme to the other, which is rather how I felt about Orkney. I'm very glad I went, and given the opportunity I'd recommend it, in fact I'm sorry I didn't get chance to explore further north and see Kirkwall, the largest settlement on the island. It was the little things that amused me, such as all the items in the small supermarket in St.Margarets Hope featuring stick on prices, or little notes that it was 'past its sell by date but still fine.' Everybody of course knew everybody else, which I can see could be the best, and worst thing about living in such a small place. I just find it fascinating, and while I don't think such a remote existence is for me, I'd like to try it for a few months perhaps.

Friday morning, and learning my lesson from the previous days crossing, I chose to sit outside under the beautiful blue skies for the crossing back to the mainland. This proved to be a good decision as the crossing was much rougher this time, in fact more and more people joined me on the top deck as our journey continued. Coming armed with a packet of Skittles to eat seemed to help too, and I was feeling absolutely fine when we docked at Gills Bay. All that stood between me and the B&B I'd booked in Wick, was a quick and easy 18 mile dash.

The dash turned out to be neither quick, nor easy. All I wanted to do was get to Wick, find my B&B, have some dinner, then go to sleep in a real bed. But no, Scotland wouldn't let me. Despite the fact my road was reasonably flat, I ended up walking for miles as the wind battered me, relentlessly. This was unlike any wind I'd encountered on the trip so far. At one point while pushing Bants along, a gust hit the side of the bike so hard that it just pushed me over into the verge. It was simply impossible. To compound matters, the weather was on the turn, plus I couldn't get any data on my phone, so other than my B&B being in Wick on Northcote street I didn't really know where to go. Putting that particular problem off until later, I fought on, with the wind finally giving in somewhat a few miles before Wick. Finally me and Bants were covering some ground again! Oh, except we didn't know where to go now we were in Wick. A quick phone call to Mum and I had a vague grasp of where to go, aided by Wick being at least a little familiar after my visit to the hospital back in July. Soon passing the hospital, and I knew I must be getting close to my bed for the night, very close in fact as I went sailing past my turning! After a quick turnaround I was on the right road and soon checked into the wonderful Netherby B&B. No sooner had I closed the door behind me, I took one glance at the plush inviting bed before collapsing on it. Nearly dozing off instantly, it took immense effort to make myself get up, shower, and stroll down into town in search of dinner. But it was so worth it. So worth it that after dinner I had two desserts, followed by chips on the way back to the B&B! Well it had been a busy fortnight, and I looked worryingly thin. In truth I'd have liked to have been carrying a little more weight at the start of the trip, but just hadn't managed it. Starting out pretty thin anyway was never going to end well, it just didn't seem possible to get enough calories in during the day, and I was showing it. I'd need to be eating well for a while to put this right I thought, as I tucked into my chips. Not the worst problem to have.

18 HOME!

Waking up in a warm bed, in a warm house, then having a nice cooked breakfast, struck me as a rather easier start to the morning than my previous ones. More B&B's would have made this trip easier. After finishing breakfast and retrieving Bants from the shed in the garden, all I had to do was cycle half a mile to Wick train station. Wick train station which appeared to be closed, as I peered through the glass doors. Hmm. The train was visible on the platform, and due to go reasonably soon, it definitely being the right train as Wick sits at the end of the line. I spotted a handful of people get onto the train. How had they done that? Following the road around to the side of the station and through a carpark showed me how, there were no doors this side, I was able to walk right onto the platform. With this being a smaller train, there was no separate carriage for bikes, instead just a small area for two, between two of the carriages. Securing Bants out of the way as best I could, I just hoped nobody else wanted to add a bike, as with all his panniers sticking out, Bants was taking up quite a lot of space.

Finding an empty seat was easy as the train left Wick, so I settled back and resumed the audio book I'd started on the trip down to Cornwall a fortnight earlier. As the miles slowly passed, and with them, tiny station after tiny station, the train became crowded. Being a Saturday, a lot of the passengers were on their way to the football, and in good spirits. Very loud good spirits, as songs and chants blared out, and a wig was placed on the good spirited conductor. I'd been joined at my table by a few rather quieter people on their way to Inverness for a day of shopping. As we chatted, I told them about my trip, and once they found out it was for charity, they all reached into their pockets to sponsor me. Kind people!

When the train finally reached Inverness, by far the biggest station I'd had to negotiate on the trip, I quickly found my way to Bants, unbuckled him, and carried him out onto the platform. Once there, and after finding my way out of the station, I set about trying to figure out what direction I'd need to be going in next. There were still a few hours to kill before I could technically pick up my hire car, but I decided to chance getting there early, to see if it was ready. If not, I'd head back into town for some lunch, as it didn't seem too far on the map. Lucky me, and despite arriving at the car hire place several hours early, my car was indeed ready! This was great news, as I still had 600 miles to cover before getting home. It would be much easier to get the journey done in one day, rather than have to find somewhere to stay on Saturday night, before completing the journey on Sunday morning. I was worried about wedging Bants, who was by this point utterly filthy, into a brand new car but the assistant told me not to worry in the slightest, that's why they employed valeters! Worry over, and having stripped Bants of his wheels and panniers, he fitted into the car well.

After programming 'home' into the satnav, I found my way out of Inverness and marvelled at just how quickly the miles were now passing. Although I find car journeys incredibly boring when I'm a passenger, I can quite happily sit and drive all day long. Plus, seeing as I was driving a new car, there were all sorts of toys and gadgets to help pass the time!

The journey was great, with only a couple fuel stops and minimal traffic, it was 11pm when I pulled into my driveway, turned off the engine, and let out a sigh. Home. This place had seemed so far away at certain points during the trip, ridiculously like I'd never get back here again. Yet now I was. Bringing everything into the house took a few trips, and once done I could only stare at the muddy pile of belongings that had gotten me through the previous few weeks. Well done Bants, well done, but now I'm going to bed, my wonderful wonderful bed. Job done.

19 THAT'S THAT THEN

So that was it. Land's End to John O'Groats by bike, an amazing experience that I'll never forget. It is strange though, for a week or so everyone you meet wants to talk about it, until you're literally all talked out on the subject, and then naturally it gets kind of forgotten. Even by yourself. But then every now and then it hits you, 'Hey, you cycled a thousand miles to John O'Groats on your own', and that's a pretty cool thought to be able to have cross your mind. Plus I've always found that completing any form of challenge, gives you an increase in confidence, for a small while at least. There just seems to be a thought of, well that seemed impossible, yet I managed it, so why can't I do whatever random thing I might be worried about now. It does wear off though unfortunately.

No matter what else I do, I'll always be proud of my little achievement. Sure thousands of people do the same every year, often faster, or easier, and people get disheartened by that, but they shouldn't. Be proud of the things you do. As you're reading this book, it's a fair guess that you're a cyclist yourself. Perhaps you've completed the same journey as me, and perhaps if so, you could see a lot of the problems I was going to encounter, before they'd happened! Maybe you've done a longer trip even, or perhaps you've read this book as you're thinking of completing the Land's End to John O'Groats trip yourself. If you're still unsure, let me tell you this. Do it. Yes there were hard days, and plenty of times when I'd have given my right arm to be anywhere but on that bike in the middle of nowhere, but those times pass, and what you're left with are the good memories, the sense of achievement, and a little more belief that you can do anything. Go on, have an adventure.

Top Tips

Be prepared for things to go wrong – Don't fear it, just accept it. There are days when everything will seem to be against you. No amount of planning can avoid this. Just work your way through each problem, one at a time, and it'll come back to you.

Plan, but don't over plan – Too many people plan everything to the 10th degree, down to every last minute detail. Some people even get so engrossed in planning that they never actually get around to doing the trip. Sure, plan a little bit, that's just sensible. Work out travel arrangements, try and outline a route, and make sure you have a phone with you at all times. But past that, just go and enjoy yourself. It'll be more fun that way, trust me.

Don't try and answer 100 texts a day – If you're lucky, people you know will be interested in your trip. This is great, and when you get back it's a pleasure when someone comes up to you and is really interested in what you've seen, experienced, how you felt, how you did it etc. Sometimes the most interested people are often the people you'd least expect too, while others who you'd think would want to know, just gloss right over it. This is fine. Just don't get so engrossed in updating a whole host of people, every hour of every day, about what's going on. You'll be tired, struggling, and missing out on the experience anyway. The best thing I did was keep my trip quiet. As soon as I posted on Facebook when I got home, my phone exploded, I loved everyone that rang or messaged me, but it would have just been too many people to deal with on a daily basis. Keeping it small, a few people who knew, always there for support or to cheer me up on a rubbish day, was the absolute best thing about my trip.

Use whatever bike you like – Don't feel that you have to waste thousands of pounds on a bespoke touring bike. Unnecessary. My bike is one of the most unsuited you could hope to use and it performed perfectly. Use what you're comfortable with, just make sure it's well serviced and performing well when you leave.

People are nice – They really are. You'll be genuinely surprised by how many nice people you meet. Cyclists are so much more approachable than car drivers, and my trip restored my faith that the world is mostly full of nice people.

Pack light – Be sensible with your packing. Pack the essentials but only the essentials, remember you're going to have to carry everything with you at all times. Multi-purpose items are amazing, use as many of these as possible. Also, weigh everything, sometimes you can find two items which perform the same task, but one weights twice as much as the other! Weigh everything, weight is a killer.

Have fun – Remember this is supposed to be fun. Yes there will be plenty of times which are more like a nightmare, but generally speaking, try and enjoy yourself.

THANKS

Thanks for reading my book. I don't profess to be a writer, and I'm certain there are many people in this world who could have made a far better job of this story than myself. That said, I wanted the words to be my own, and to get across the feelings and emotions I felt during my time alone with Bants. I hope you enjoyed the insight into my strange mind. If there's anything else you'd like to know, please feel free to contact me, it would be a pleasure to hear from you. Or, you know, a review on Amazon would also be much appreciated!

As for me, with this adventure complete, I've started eyeing up the next one. It's a big one. America. More specifically the Trans-America trail, the classic 4228 mile route across America. Bants is already shaking at the thought of it…wish us luck!

Cycle safe, Ross

E-mail- rossloram@tiscali.co.uk

Printed in Great Britain
by Amazon

60902871R00112